MW01622756

No Hair Day

No Hair Day

Dessie Dorsey

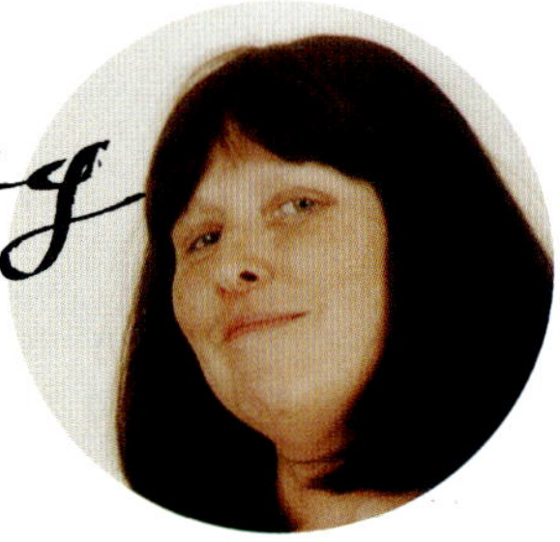

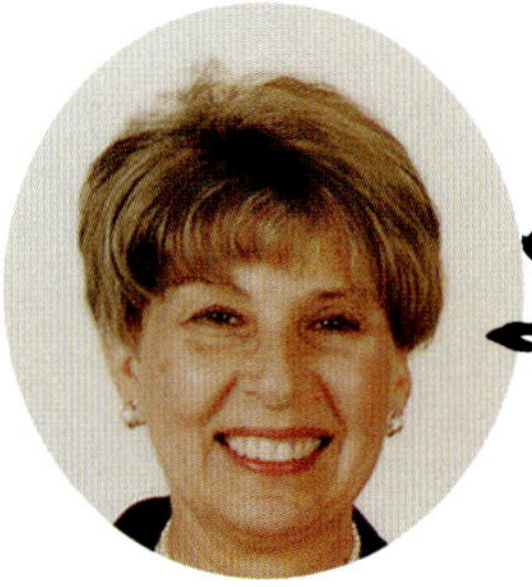

Lissy Levinson

Carol Potoff

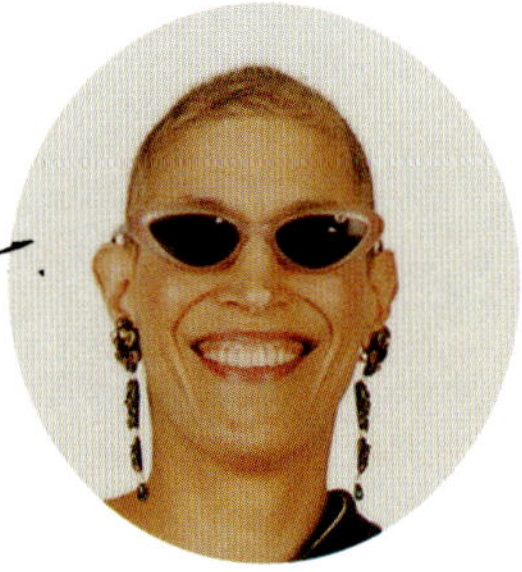

A Collaboration

by

Elsa Dorfman

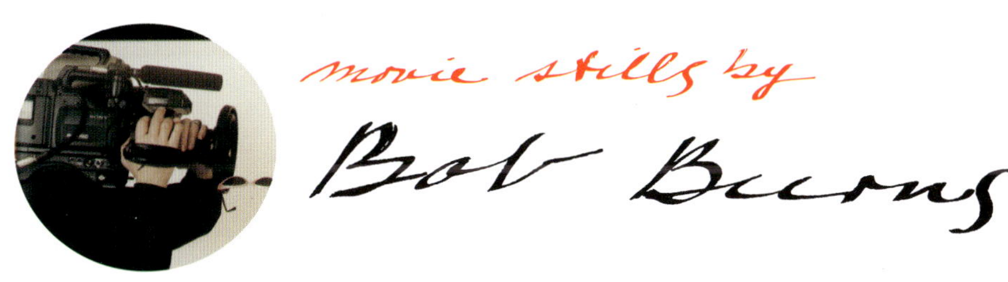

movie stills by

Bob Burns

ISBN 0-9668665-0-9

Entire book available at **WWW.ELSA.PHOTO.NET**

Designed by Katy Homans

First Published 2003
Printed on acid-free paper
Printed and bound in Hong Kong

Distributed to the trade by **WWW.ELSA.PHOTO.NET**
607 Franklin St.
Cambridge, MA 02139-2923
Orders: T:617-876-6416 F:617-492-4925
email:elsad@theworld.com

Cambridge Studios
www.nohairday.com
No Hair Day, the movie, is a Cambridge Studios Production
in association with WGBH/Boston.

For my dear subjects who feared the end was near and for love of their family and friends came to my studio.

TERRY ARTMAN
JIM BEGIN
HERMAN BUDNICK
BRUCE CRATSLEY
CAROLINE RIGBY GRABOYS
CONSTANCE GRICE
PAUL HIRSHSON
JOHN HOMANS
DARCIE KAROL
BERNADETTE LEHR
KEVIN HYNES
CLAIRE McKEOWN
CAROL POTOFF
MARY C. RAUGUST
MARC SAWYER
NANCY SILVERMAN
LEONARD P. ZAKIM
SUSAN WISE

and for my friend R.Michael Kirchmayer who hopefully didn't see the 1995 Toyota that hit him at 1:38 a.m. on December 25, 1998 near the intersection of NE 4th Avenue and NE 15th Street in Ft. Lauderdale, FL.

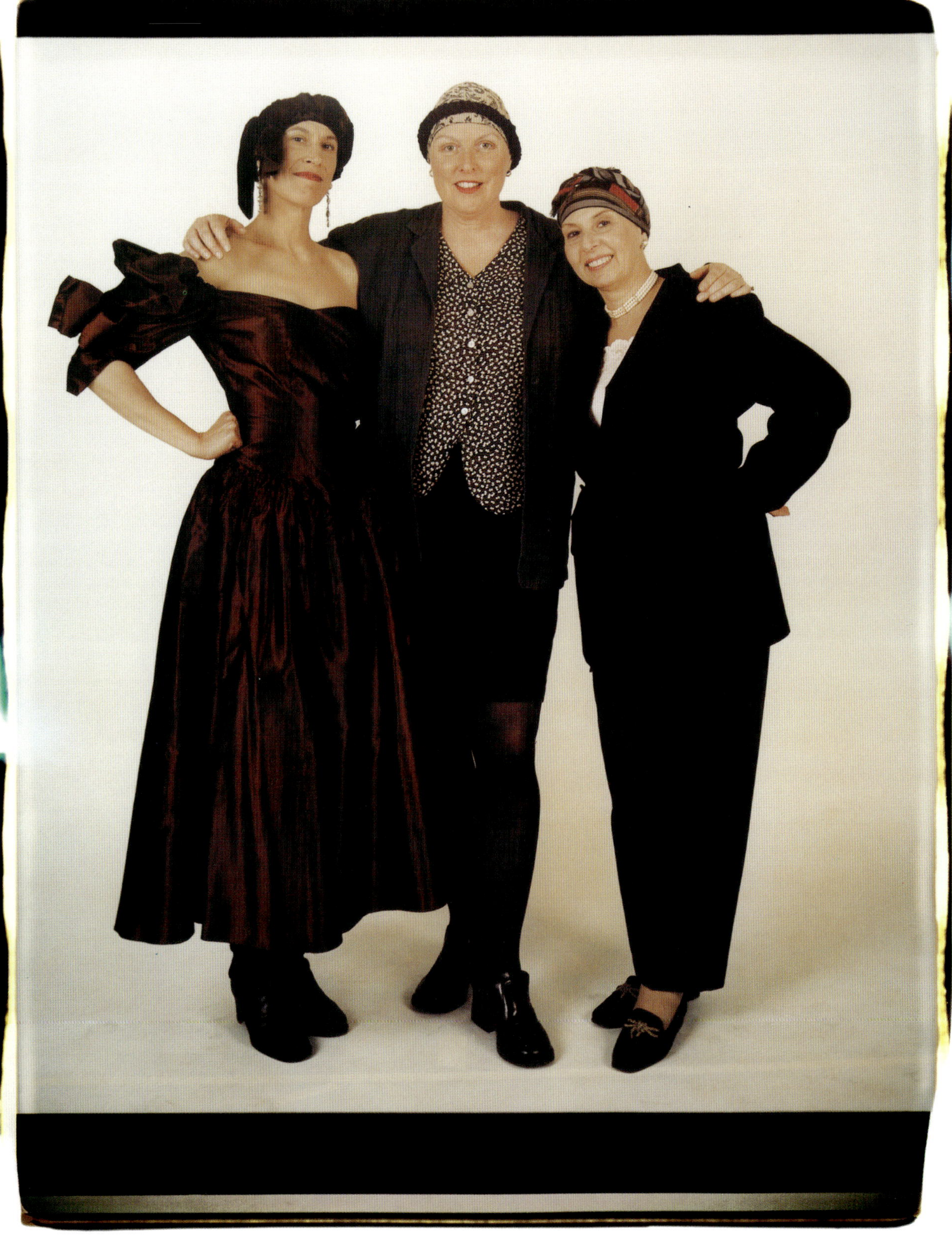

How It Happened

ELSA THERE WERE SEVEN OF US AND TWO CAMERAS. Debbie Dorsey, Carol Potoff and Libby Levinson were the three STARS. Bob Burns, Debbie's husband and a film maker, shot video. He worked with Terry Rockefeller who did sound. I shot with the Polaroid 20 x 24. Debra Ciolfi, Debbie's longtime friend, was an extra pair of hands. None of us knew what was going to happen.

We were all here because Debbie, a film maker and film editor I'd met when I'd photographed her a few years ago, had called me out of the blue. She said she had been diagnosed with breast cancer, was going through radiation, and wanted to do something to take her mind off what she was going through. She wondered if I had any ideas.

It didn't take long to come up with a plan. I would take some portraits of Debbie and Bob Burns would film the session. Debbie said she had two friends she had made while figuring out the chemo world, Libby Levinson and Carol Potoff, who also would be up for the portrait-making. Libby is an administrator at a computer publishing company and Carol is an artist and high school art teacher.

We picked a shoot date, March 12, 1998, when I would meet Libby and Carol for the first time. I knew I wanted HOPE in the pictures. I didn't want SHAME and I didn't want FEAR. I wanted FUN. I wanted DARING. Not

BOB BURNS Debbie losing her hair was so very traumatic. I can't tell you how many times we were lying in bed talking about how difficult it was for her to lose her hair and to be bald. Being bald makes it impossible for you to ignore that you have cancer. You can't put it aside. You can't pretend that you don't. You just do.

Seeing Debbie—in those photographs and especially where she's holding up the wig and smiling at the same time with such a great laugh—was great. It was hard for me to hold the camera still.

Debbie kept talking about wanting to make a tv show, a tv show about having cancer. And I kept putting it off, not wanting to do it, not being that interested in it. But when she actually called Elsa and made this thing happen, then I said, Jeez, something special could happen there. Let's just go and shoot it. We didn't even really know we were going to do it till the day of the shoot, you know, the kids weren't sick so they were going to go to school, and I didn't have another job that day, I had nothing else I had to do. And all the equipment was working. So, yeah, let's do it.

Frankly, I did it partially as a way of helping myself deal with it. Debbie deals with things by talking about them again and again and again and again. I'm a guy. I talk about things once or twice, and then, you know, I'm done. Making a project out of it, making a film is a way, in one sense, of dealing with it.

Debbie's brush with death focused me on the notion of death, too. But it's something as a society we deal with badly, and we need to do better. We need to take that and make death present every day, because it really is always there, and it doesn't have to be such a thing to be scared of. If you know that it's there every day. . . . The light could fall down on me, and I'd be dead. That's not likely, but it's there. And if I know that the light can fall down on me and I would be dead, then I can say, just say what I'm feeling and not worry about it, because it might be the last thing I ever say.

just daring the cancer but daring the camera to work. No breakdowns. I had done portraits of people who knew they were dying, portraits of people who hoped they weren't dying. Four portraits of young mothers with breast cancer and their families. Friends with AIDS. They were all with me during the NoHairDay shoot.

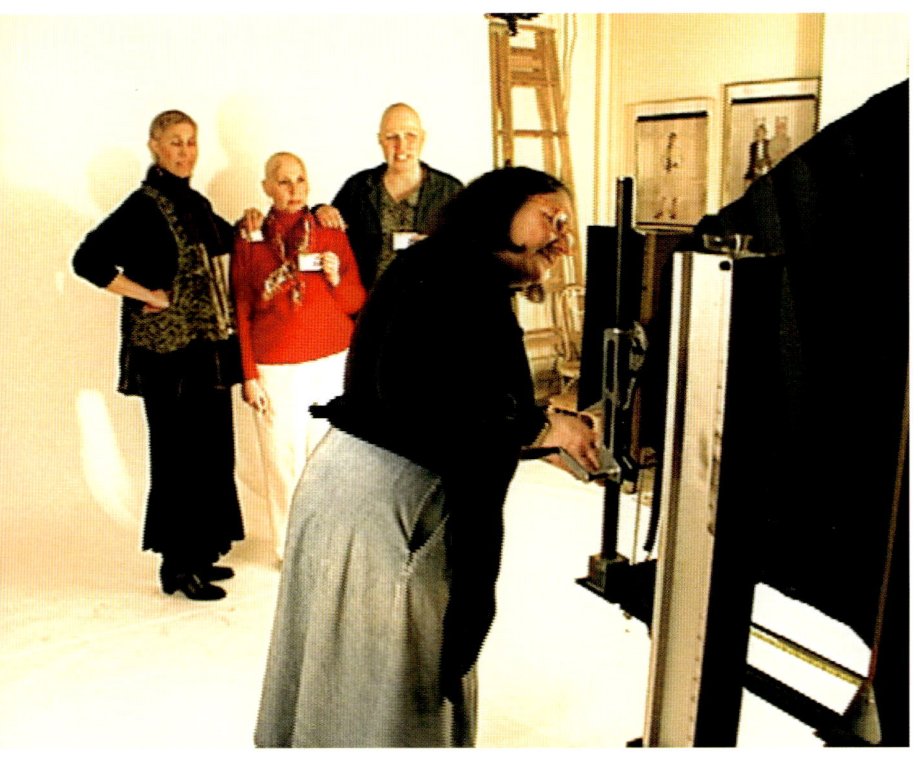

The first thing we did on the day of the shoot was order pizza and soda from Il Panino down the street and look at the props I'd asked the women to bring. Debbie, Carol and Libby had brought hospital nightgowns, chemo vials, food coloring, books about breast cancer, glamorous dresses, baseball caps, turbans galore, wigs. And we talked and talked. I hadn't seen Debbie and Bob Burns in seven years. They had been given a wedding present of a portrait by me from friends and had finally used it when their son Bobby was eighteen months. Now they also have a little girl, Georgia.

Libby had come with her patient ID number, cardboard and a color marker. She had the sense that the pictures probably had to be depressing, and wanted to hold her ID number across her chest, like a person in prison. She wanted to wear an ugly, shapeless nightgown. But I didn't want to make a portrait in which she looked ugly or angry or down. So I began by taking a portrait of where we were: eating pizza.

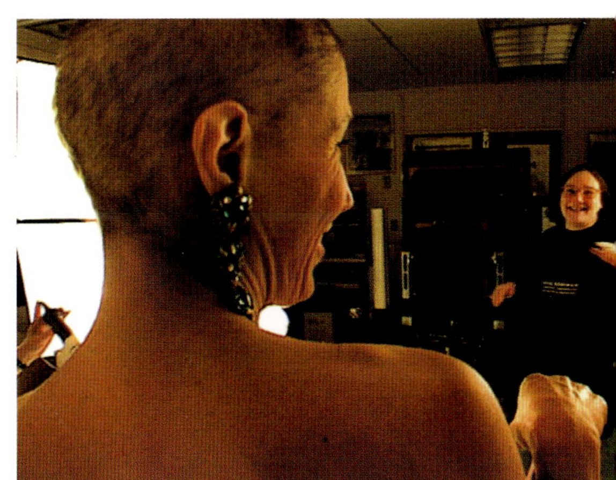

One image led to another. Because I work with the Polaroid 20 x 24 camera we could see the photo 70 seconds after I clicked the shutter. There it was in all its clarity and color and dramatic size: 23 x 36 inches. We got more and more excited. The little miracles thrilled us; the camera worked; no one blinked, I didn't forget to pull down the negative. Absolutely nothing went wrong.

Libby, who'd had a complete mastectomy, Carol, who'd had a partial mastectomy and reconstruction, and Debbie, who'd had a lumpectomy, became increasingly frank and daring in front of the camera.

Bob Burns and Terry Rockefeller were documenting our every word and every move, adding to our energy. Occasionally, they would ask us questions on camera.

CAROL TALKS ABOUT ELSA Elsa is so down to earth and she seems to enjoy the shoot as much as we did. Here she is, wrapped in her head dress. We tied her head up, you know, wrapped her head too. Oh she was lovely. . . it was so sweet of her to do that. It really boosted my spirits. What a crew! Are we gorgeous or what? I don't know, I expected some hotsie totsie photographer person and there was Elsa, this short Jewish woman, and I thought, wait a minute, that's not anything like I expected. It was great.

I think she really catches a slice of life. She takes the picture and whatever the camera catches, it catches. You know, there's no polishing it up or making any changes. What you see, what's there, is what you get. That's it, boom, done. You got your eyes closed? Well that's how it comes out. Whatever—it's there. There's an honesty to her work that you don't get elsewhere.

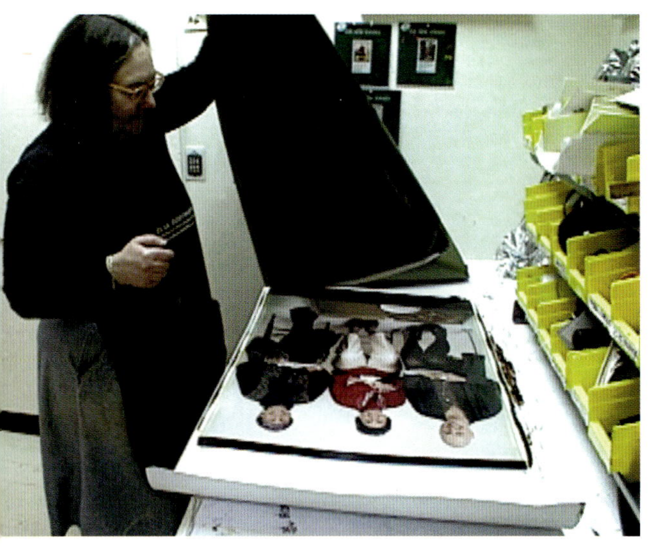

As I pinned up each sequential picture on my studio board so that we could examine it, we came up with the next pose simultaneously. We were all on the same wave.

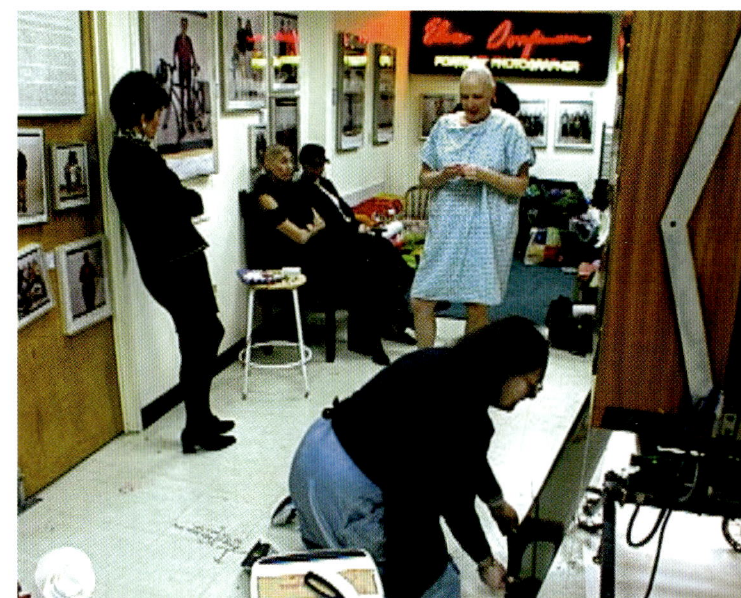

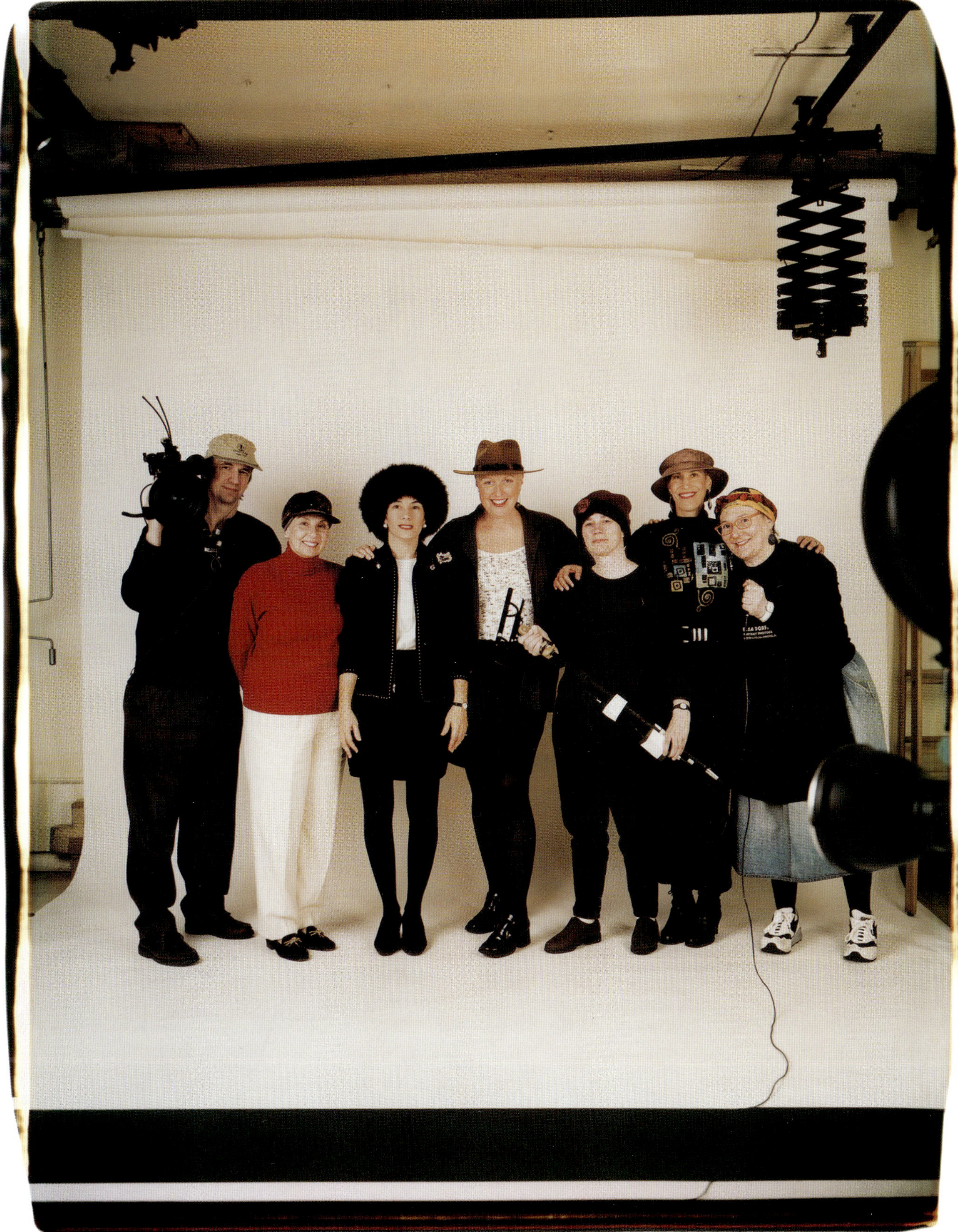

DEBBIE One day Carolyn Krusinski came over and told me that I should call the artist who took the large Polaroid of my family and ask her to take my picture bald. I laughed and thought, why not. Elsa answered the phone and I said Elsa you don't remember me but you took my picture with my husband and son about seven years ago. My name is Debbie Dorsey. She said oh I remember you. Then I said Elsa I'm going to give you a gift. I'm going to give you three bald women who are undergoing chemotherapy for breast cancer. You should take our picture. There was a pause and then Elsa said cool, let's do it. I'm not busy in the winter.

I called Libby thinking she would never want to do it. But when I told her that Elsa wanted to take our picture she jumped on it. Libby and I talked for hours about how we were never comfortable enough to go without a wig. When we went out chemo-chic with a scarf and a baseball cap, we thought we were really daring.

Then I called Carol who said why not. I've had cancer. I can do anything. Carol never wore a wig, and most of the time she didn't wear anything unless it was cold. Being an artist, Carol really got into what we should bring. She gathered gowns, dozens of scarves and material for turbans. Her favorite color is purple.

Before the shoot at Elsa's, Libby and I visited Carol on her last day of a hospital stay because her white blood cells had dropped too low. I said that if we were going to do the photographs with Elsa we had better get used to the three of us being bald. So we all crammed into Carol's bathroom and Libby and I took off our wigs. We each looked at each other's bald head and started laughing. Carol had a little hair that was pretty dark so she didn't look too bad. Libby was bald except for little strands of hair here and there. She called them her porcupine hairs. I was shocked because it was the first time that I realized how bald I really was. We compared the amount of hair we didn't have. We examined the shape of our heads.

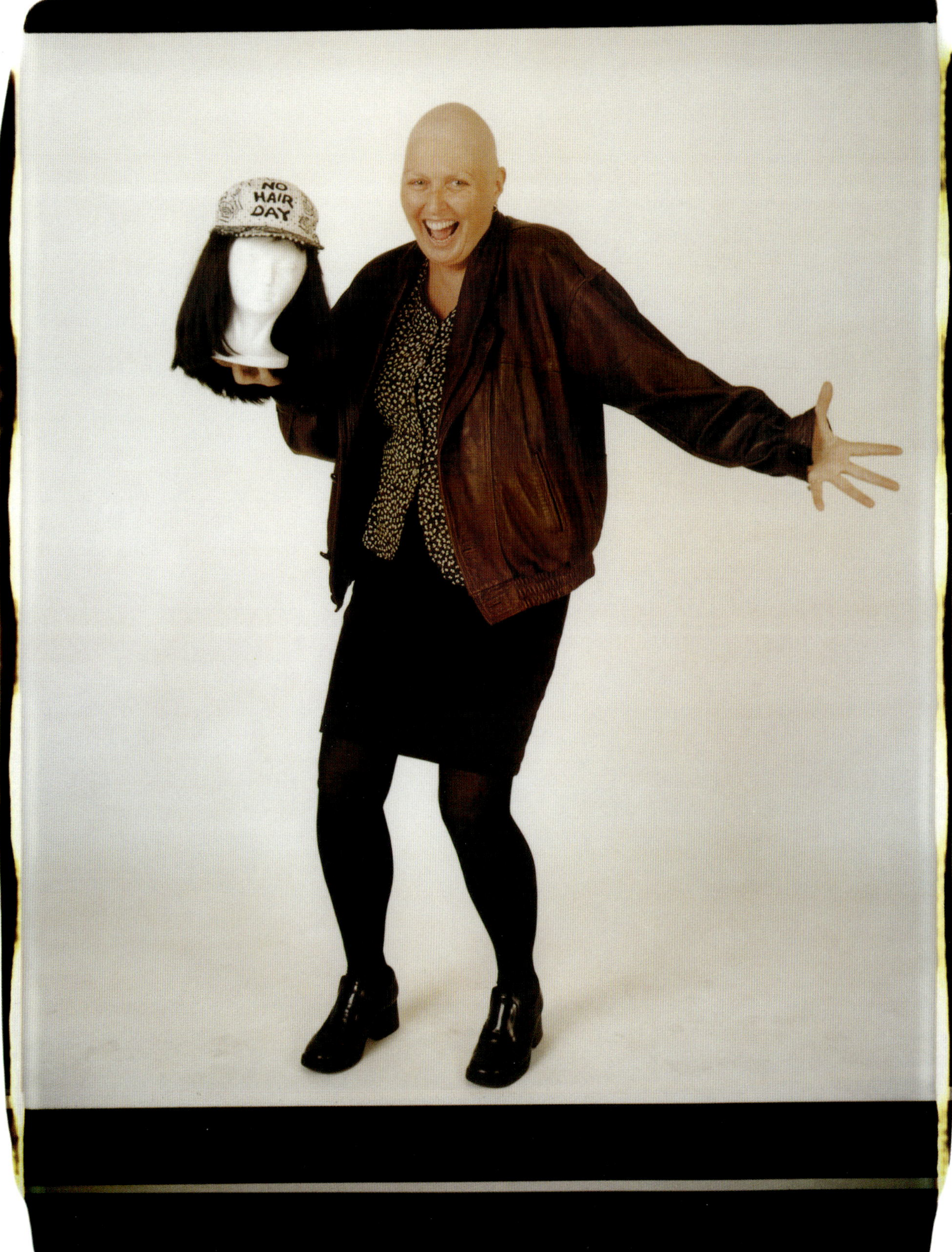
NO
HAIR
DAY

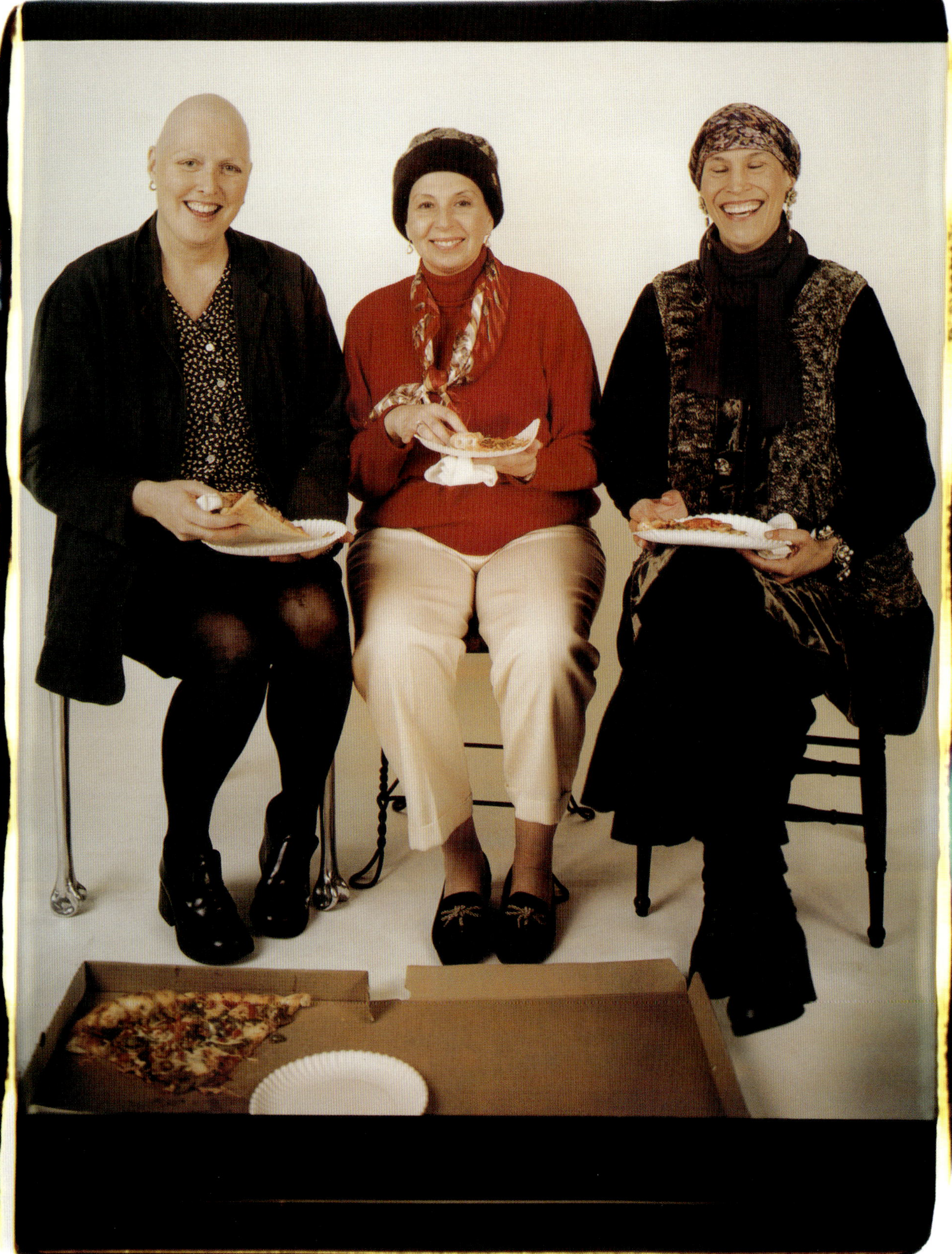

Starting with Pizza

ELSA Carol, you move in a crumb. Okay. Debbie, you have to move in a crumb. Just a real crumb.

CAROL Sit up straight. I can hear my mother. Sit up straight.

ELSA No, no, no, you don't. So, wait a minute. All right. I just wanted to make sure it was in focus. That's the thing about this camera. Okay. All right. Now we're ready.

[OVERLAPPING VOICES]

ELSA Now we're ready. Now we're ready. All right. Shh. All right. Now we're ready.

DEBBIE What if we have pizza on our teeth or something?

CAROL I think I do. What do you mean, what if?

ELSA That would be good. Okay. So, look right at the lens. Okay, here goes. You ready? Okay. That's good. Okay. Look right here. Okay. Good. All right. So now you can continue eating and I'm going to process the picture.

[70 SECONDS LATER ELSA PULLS APART THE POSITIVE AND THE NEGATIVE]

DEBBIE Mmm-hmm. Oh, my God!

[LAUGHTER]

CAROL Oh, my eyes are closed!

ELSA I know, but it's great. It's great.

LIBBY That is actually great.

CAROL That's a riot.

DEBBIE This is really funny. Pizza.

ELSA Yeah. It's good.

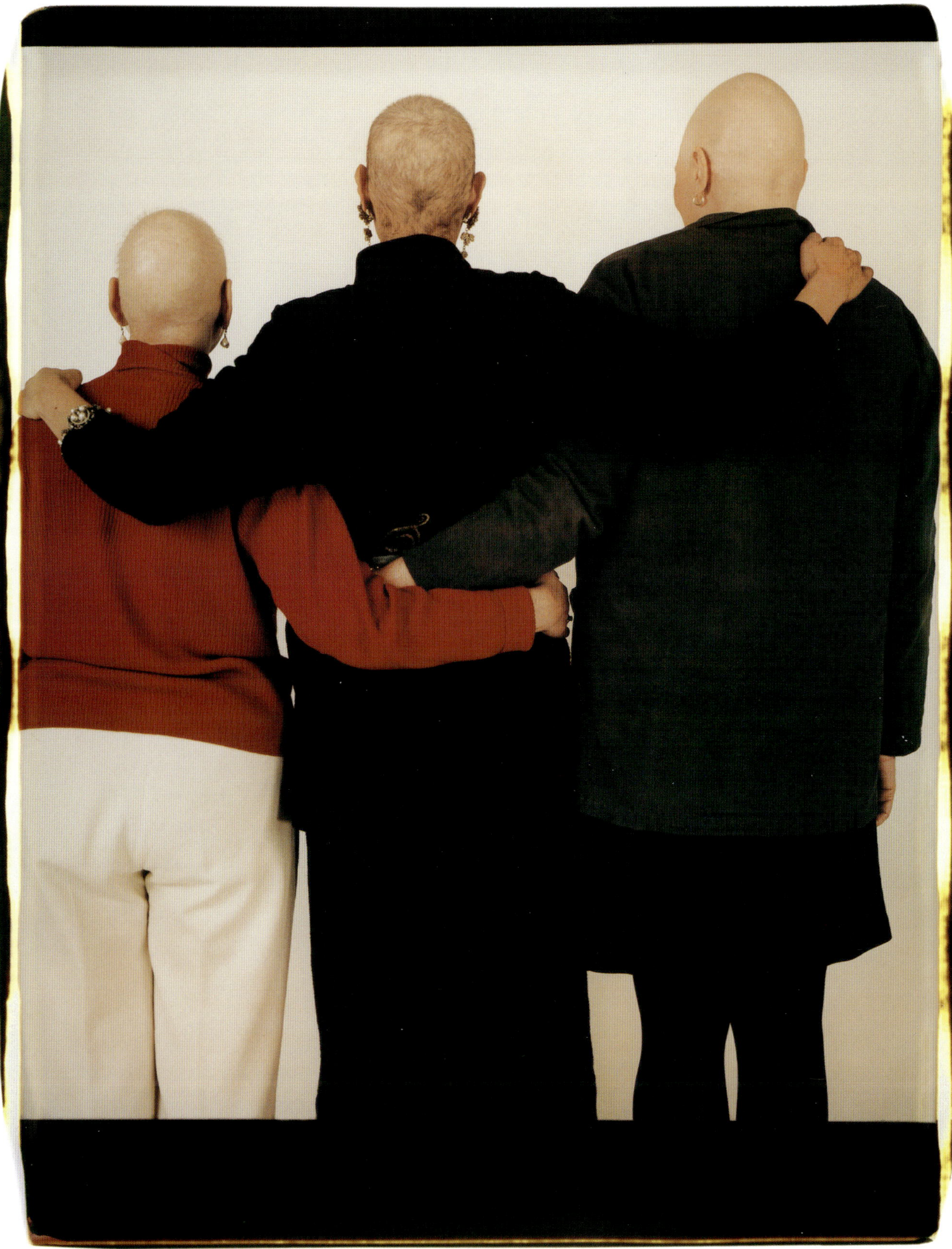

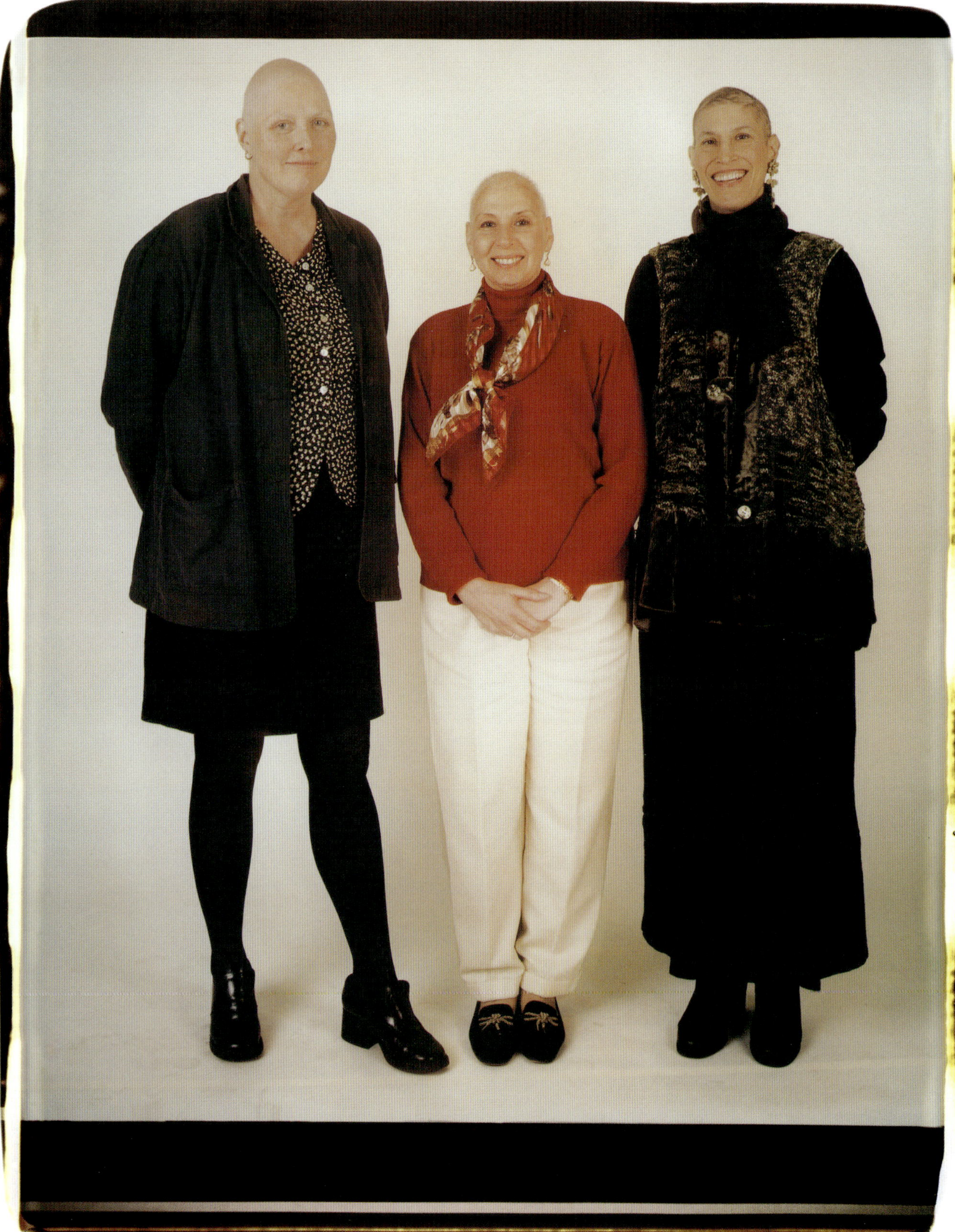

CAROL It is funny.

ELSA Okay.

CAROL We're looking good. It was the pizza that did it.

LIBBY And we're just getting warmed up.

ELSA Right, You're just getting warmed up.

DEBBIE We're just getting warmed up.

ELSA Next, I guess, after we eat, we should do the three of you bald.

CAROL Okay.

ELSA Front and back. Okay.

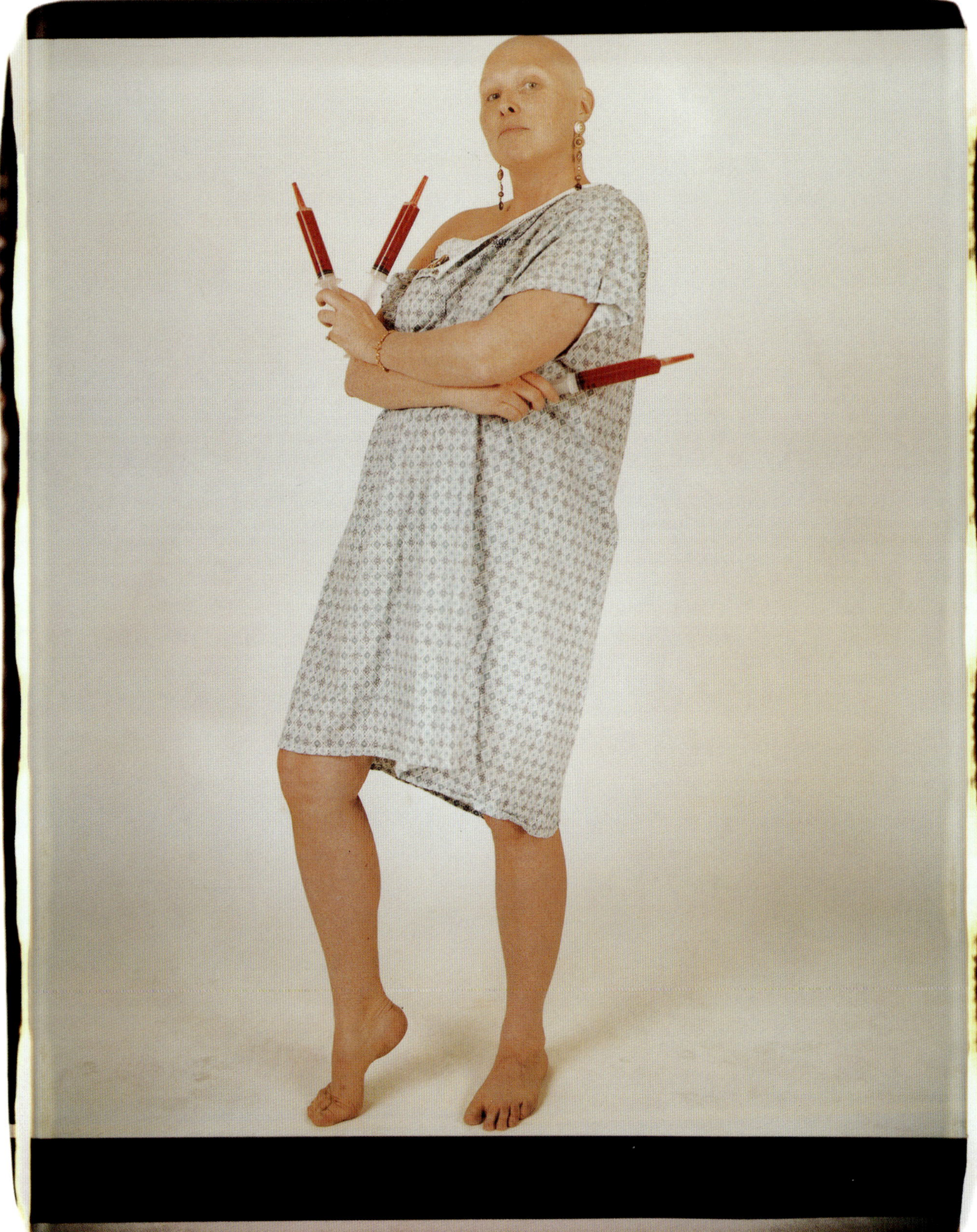

Dessie Dorsey

I WAS COMPLETELY FREAKED OUT WHEN MY HAIR GREW BACK CURLY. I couldn't believe it. I had very long, dark, straight hair. It had maybe a little bit of curl but it grew back and it's continuing to be very, very curly, which is really kind of ironic because when I was a little girl, that's all I dreamed of, having long, curly hair.

When my hair started growing back and it was growing back curly, I met some woman on the street and she said, Oh! I love your hair! Where did you get it done? And I said, Oh, I got it done at Dana Farber Cancer Institute. So I kind of shocked her, and I apologized: Sorry, I didn't mean to say that, but it was pretty funny, your asking me like that.

On October 23, 1997 I was diagnosed with breast cancer. It was pretty dramatic and traumatic and pretty devastating, and it changed my life a lot.

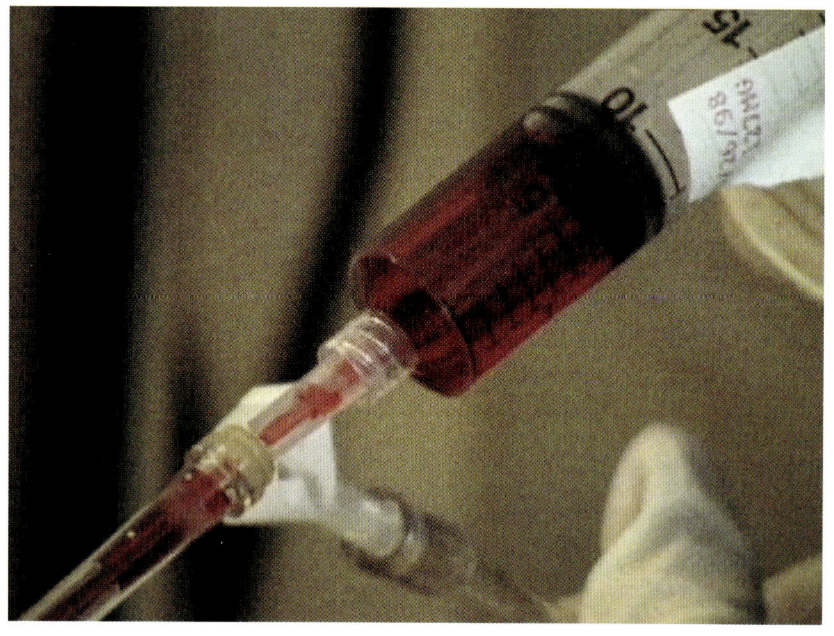

I don't know why, but when I was younger, I always wondered how a doctor would tell somebody that they had cancer. Would they come in and say you have cancer, or oh, I'm sorry, you have cancer, or would they come in and say oh, no, things aren't too good, it's not good.

When I was told, it was after a biopsy. I had been told by two breast surgeons that it did not look like cancer, that it was not cancer, that it was this lump in my right breast, but I should get it out because who wants a lump in their right breast? So, I went into the hospital and had a biopsy. During the biopsy, the surgeon said, Oh, this looks good, this looks great. I wasn't stressed because I wasn't worried about anything. I thought this was nothing, I was going to be fine. I was actually talking to one of the nurses about a facelift, like, would I ever get one some day. She had just had a beautiful facelift.

I went into the recovery room and sat there for a while talking to all the other patients and asking what their diseases or ailments were. Then a nurse came in and said, the doctor wants to see you, and I said, is everything okay? She said oh, yeah. I said okay.

So, I went into this tiny, excruciatingly tiny room. There was my Bob. I looked at him and I said, It seemed like it went fine. Do you know anything? He said, No. All of a sudden the door opened and Barbara Smith, who is my surgeon, she just kind of like bent down and she said, Well, some of the cells were cancerous.

And I just looked at her. I said, What are you telling me? Are you telling me I have breast cancer? And she said, Yeah. And I just, I mean, it was amazing. It was like my whole world just stopped. It just stopped cold. Like I couldn't hear anything. I couldn't hear the people talking. I just went, oh my God.

Because cancer, you know. Cancer equals death. A lot of people get cancer and die. And the idea of getting it is just terrifying. There are a lot of women who make it, but there are a lot of women out there and a lot of men who don't make it. And it's not just breast cancer. It's all different types of cancer. So, after she told me, I had to go get dressed and I walked out into the hall and the nurse who had the facelift came up to me, and she said, So, you're okay. You're all right. Everything's good, right? And I looked at her and I said, No. No. It's not good. Her face went completely down.

And I said, "Oh, my God. I'm so sorry. I'm so sorry. I'm sorry."

That was the beginning of the apologies. I apologized to everybody. I apologized to my husband. I apologized to people at work. I apologized to my friends because I thought it was me, was my fault.

I must have done something wrong. I must have not taken enough care of myself. It was probably because I smoked cigarettes. It might be from lots of different sorts of things. Maybe it was this cleaner that I had used on the rug. But it had to be my fault. It took me a long, long time to realize that it was nothing that I did. And I know it's not my fault.

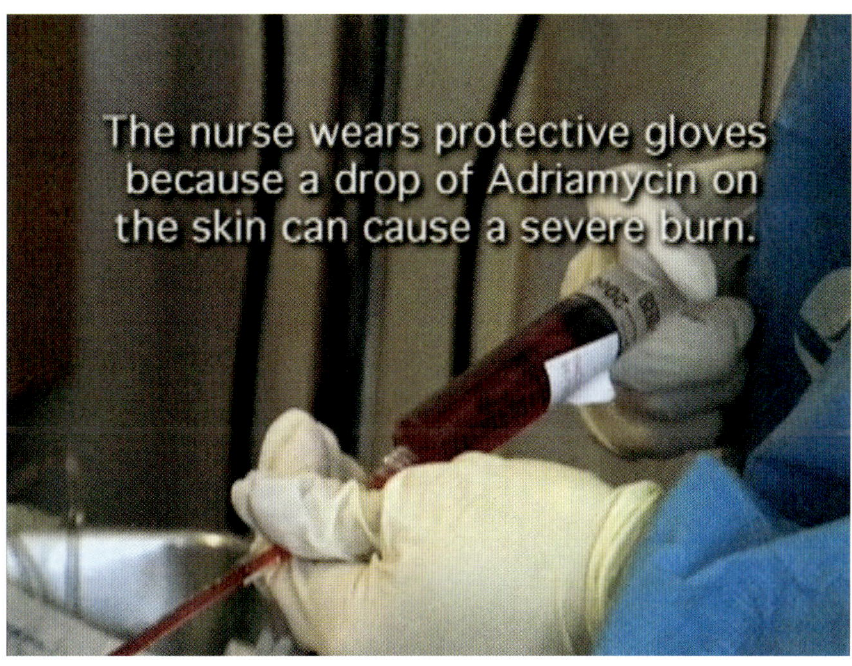

I was curious why the other women in the support group thought they got cancer. Libby said that she got cancer because she was exercising on the floor and the dog stepped on her breast. Is that ludicrous? Well, who knows?

My friend Ann Marie Bronski from my support group said the reason she thinks she got cancer is because she wore miniskirts, no bra and a lot of white lipstick in the '60s and '70s.

The point being that nobody knows. They just don't know. Every single woman who I know who has cancer would give anything to know why.

Breast cancer brings you into a whole new world. The hardest thing I ever did during that whole period of time was walking into an office with the word "oncology" over the door. I just started shaking. I just said Oh, my God.

After the doctor had told me that I indeed had breast cancer, she then told me that the lump was small, but the cells were a bit too aggressive, which was bad. I was going to need chemotherapy.

So, I said oh, bring on the chemo. This is great. I'm going to fight the good fight. This is wonderful.

Then I started thinking about it and I said, chemotherapy, chemotherapy. So I called her back and said, are you talking about the chemotherapy that makes you lose all of your hair or the chemotherapy that doesn't make you lose all your hair? She said, well, that's going to be up to your oncologist. And I said, okay.

Anyway, at Dana Farber, they have these multidisciplinary groups where the whole team meets you, the breast surgeon, the oncologist and the radiation doctor. Oncologists are funny people. Actually, Hal Bernstein, when I first met him, I asked him why do you do this? Why do you do oncology? He said it's fun, and I almost slugged him. I said what do you mean it's fun? This is fun? This is not fun at all. But after some time, I realized what he meant is that it's really fun when it works.

There were a lot of people who were really trying to calm me down. At one point, somebody said, you should go to a support group.

I said I'm not into groups. I've never done a group.

They said "You should go." I found out through a friend, Jay Hutchinson, who called a friend of hers, that there was this woman everyone called Hester, the good. She was Hester Hill at Beth Israel Hospital Cancer Institute. So, I called up Hester and said I was headed toward chemotherapy on December 10, 1997. She said come to the group.

So, that was a very hard door to walk through. I was going as slow as I could down the hall because I said I don't want to do this. I don't want to have to talk about it. I'm going to cry. This is going to be like the worst thing in the world. I walked in, I sat down, and I was just sitting there. There were about five or six other people and there was Hester. In walks this woman. She was very corporate. She was very, what do you call it, just very tailored-looking and very pretty and just, anyway, she sat down, she looked at everybody and then she started crying and said, "Why me?" And I just looked at her and said, Oh, my God. She's crying. I'm going to start crying. So I started crying.

That woman was Libby. She was my chemo buddy. We went through chemotherapy together. We didn't do it at the same places—she did hers at Beth Israel, and I was over at the Dana Farber. But we talked almost every single day on the phone. She was my lifesaver.

Talking every day on the phone to her, it was like, oh, how do you feel today? Oh, well, I'm feeling a little bad, or what's going on today, or today's a better day, and I'd say oh, that's good that today was a better day. And if I had a bad day, she's say wait a day. It was always like we were in tune. One was always stronger than the other and we could help each other. We were just incredible together.

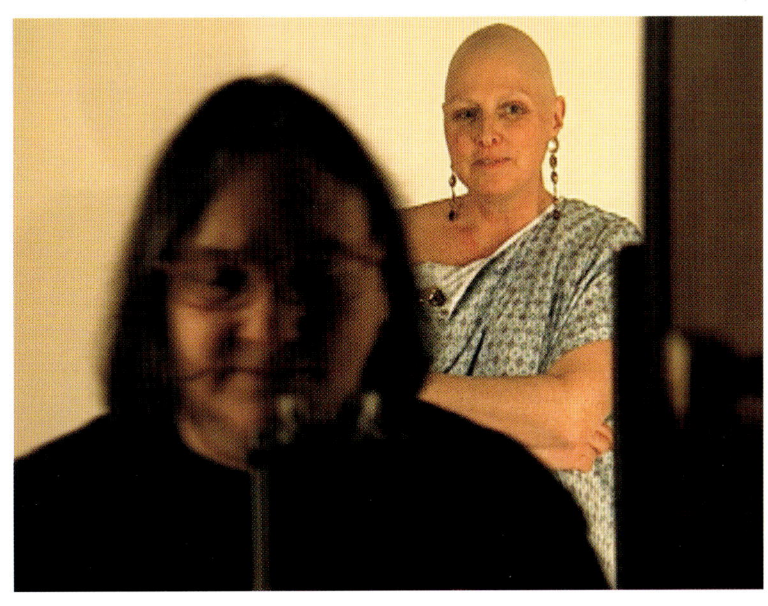

We lost all of our hair. We started talking a lot about it every day and we'd give each other support. And every day we'd go outside wearing our wigs or wearing hats or wearing a turban.

It's really interesting, when you lose your hair and you're fighting cancer, because everybody talks about fighting cancer. You've got to fight cancer. And it's okay, well, I'm going to fight cancer and I'm going to fight the good fight. And you go outside into public wearing a turban and walk into a bakery shop and, all of a sudden, people turn around and go, cancer has walked in the door.

People were terrified of me. I used to go running home and call Libby and say what's going on? You mean I'm not going to get any support for this? We couldn't figure it out, so we got really, really angry. We said okay, forget about the wigs. We're not going to wear the wigs anymore, we're just going to wear scarves. People are going to see that we're bald.

Actually, we never had enough gumption to go out in public completely bald. We never could do it. It was too scary. Some women can do it. The ones that can, I just think they're amazing, that they can do that.

Carol was one of those women who could go out in public bald. She was incredible. I met Carol at a conference for cancer, right after I had my operation, and my doctors were up on stage and they were talking. It was during a question-and-answer period. Carol got up there and asked why do I have to have a mastectomy? Why haven't you guys got the research done? Why did I get breast cancer? You guys aren't doing your job.

I went, whoa! Who is this woman? She asked what about alternative medicine? Why can't you use that? They were trying to answer her questions and stuff, and I said this woman is really interesting. So I went up to her after the conference was over and I said, my name is Debbie Dorsey, I'd love to talk to you. She lives on the Cape and I live in the Boston area. We started this long-distance telephone relationship. She's fabulous. She has so much spirit and gumption and life in her.

People think of cancer, I call it the cancer equation: cancer equals death or cancer can equal life. Getting a life-threatening disease and thinking that you're going to die all of a sudden makes you really, really appreciate life more and how important it really is and how you should really cherish each and every day. I still think there are jerks in the world, there are still lots of people I don't like, but it doesn't bother me as much in that sort of situation.

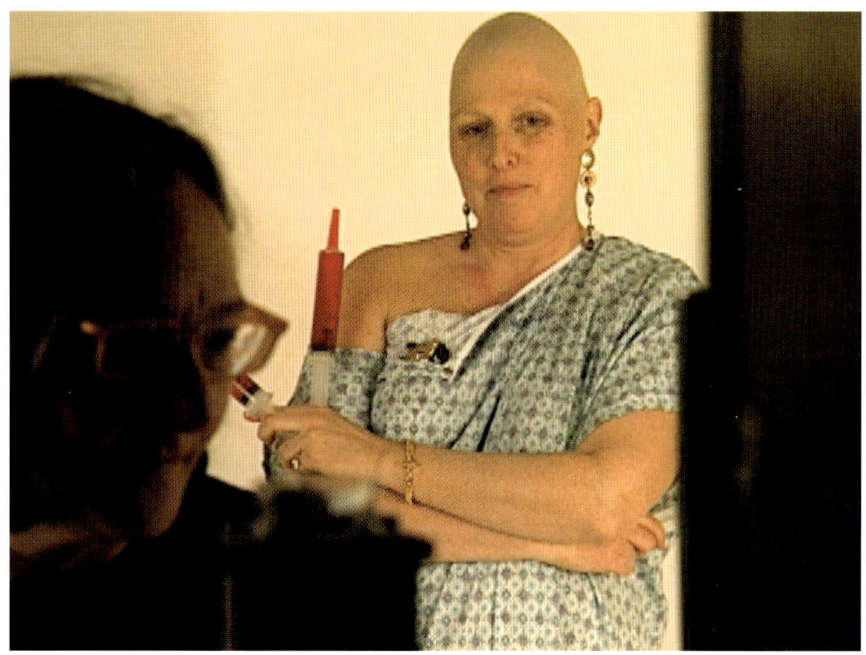

Before my hair fell out, I was very, very sad. I remember, one day, sitting on the couch and crying, sobbing. I had beautiful long, beautiful brown auburn hair. It was gorgeous. I don't think it was really auburn, maybe it was just dark, but anyway, it was gorgeous. There was just a lot of thick hair. It was wonderful and it was, like, my crowning glory.

Anyway, I was sitting on the couch and I was just sobbing. And my son Bobby walked in. He said, "Mom, why are you crying?" We were very open with Bobby, told him everything right from the start so he knew that I had cancer and stuff. And he said "Mom, why are you crying?" and I said I'm so sad. I'm going to lose all my hair. Your mother's going to be bald. It's going to be awful. He looked at me and he said "Mom, isn't it better going bald than dying?" And I just looked at him like, excuse me? How old are you? He was eight. And he just snapped me out of it. Oh, well, I guess you're right.

On December 10th, 1997 I had my first treatment of chemotherapy. Hal Bernstein and Eric Weiner said, you're going to get through this. And I said, great. I said, so what's the deal about the hair? And they said, oh, fifteen days. I said what do you mean? Oh, yeah, it'll be out in fifteen days. And I said yeah, I mean, but there is a percentage of people that aren't going to lose their hair. They said yeah, but that's very small. And I said well, maybe I'll be one of those, and Hal said fifteen days. So I went home and started tugging at my hair. Every day I would tug at my hair. I would tug and tug and tug and it wouldn't come out. Then, Christmas morning, Christmas morning I was sitting there. I remember I was sitting in the chair, we were exchanging gifts and, all of a sudden, I went tug, tug and about seven strands came out. I just looked at them and I said well, maybe I'll be one of the ones that it doesn't all fall out. Anyway, before New Years, Bob Burns and Bobbie buzzed my head. I couldn't believe it. I just couldn't believe it. I couldn't believe it when I looked at myself in the mirror and I said, Oh, my God. That's not me.

The worst part about it was that I had a pointed head. Some women have these beautiful heads, but I had to have a pointed head. I had a big, pointed head and so I wasn't too crazy about it. I just remember every single day waking up and looking at myself in the mirror and going, Oh, my God.

When I finished my treatment, a doctor spoke with me and I said what do I do now? Do I exercise or diet? How do I build up my immune system? What should I do? Tell me what I can do so that I don't have to go through this again. He said he didn't know. He said the best thing you can do, and he said I know it sounds hard, but the best thing you can do is pretend it never happened. I said, excuse me? Pretend it never happened? Two surgeries, four doses of chemotherapy and thirty-two days of radiation and it never happened to me? Yeah.

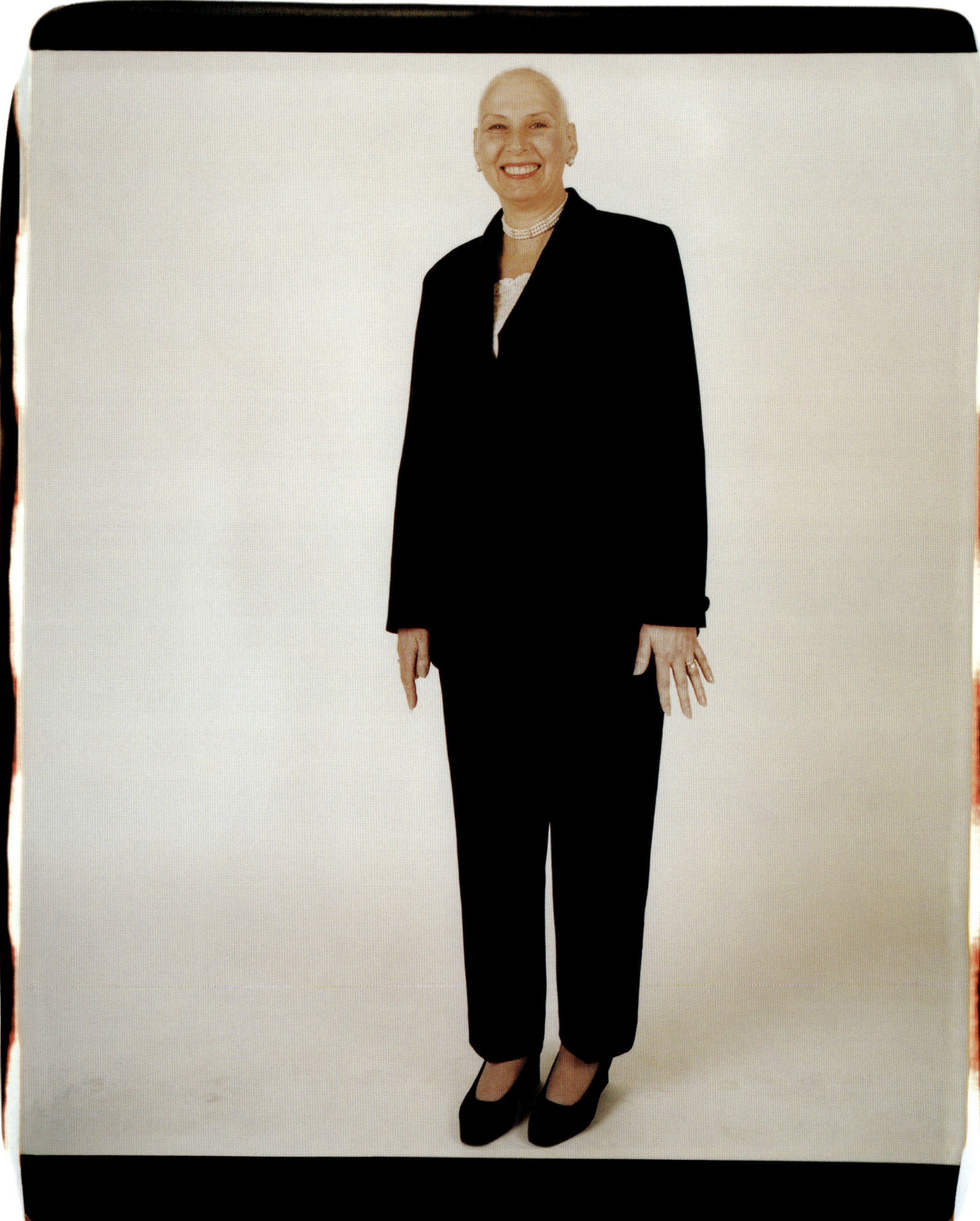

Lissy Levinson

I'M LIBBY LEVINSON AND ON NOVEMBER 5, 1997, I GOT THE GOOD NEWS THAT I HAD BREAST CANCER. I had had a routine mammogram and some calcifications were discovered on the mammogram, on my left breast. My gynecologist recommended that I see a breast surgeon, who recommended a biopsy, and I got the results of the biopsy on November 5, that I had breast cancer.

It was a very grave day. I was convinced that I didn't have breast cancer. I was reassuring the surgeon the day of the biopsy, not to worry about me, that I was fine, that my biopsy was going to be negative. I was trying to believe that, thinking that if I really, really held tight to that belief, that I wouldn't have breast cancer.

The next step was to revisit the surgeon and to discuss with him what my options were, whether to have a lumpectomy or a mastectomy, whether to have reconstruction with a mastectomy, whether to have bilateral mastectomy or just the mastectomy on the left side. I opted for the mastectomy and not the lumpectomy because there were actually two sites in the breast, two locations where they found calcifications.

Only one location had been biopsied, and of course it was positive for cancer. So I was convinced that the other location would also be cancer, and I just opted to have the breast removed rather than going and having another biopsy and having to wait another couple of days to find out whether in fact it was cancer. I couldn't live with that. I just wanted the breast off. I made up my mind right then and there in the surgeon's office. My husband was with me; my sister was with me. They were both very supportive of my decision, and I was anxious to move forward with my surgery.

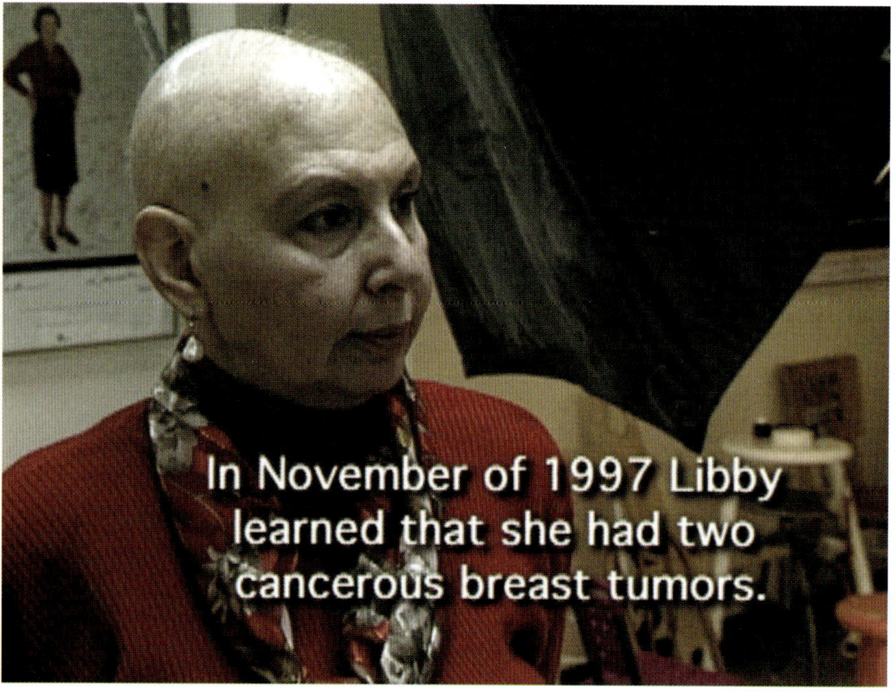

The surgeon insisted that I visit a plastic surgeon to learn about reconstructive surgery and then to make my decision as to whether I wanted it. I knew I didn't want reconstructive surgery. I just wanted to have the breast removed.

I met Debbie Dorsey at a breast cancer support group. It was exactly a week before I was scheduled to start chemotherapy. I came into the group very frightened, not knowing what to expect, not knowing what the women were going to look like, how they were going to feel. I came, sat down, and burst into tears. I introduced myself once I got my composure. I learned that there was one other woman in the group who was exactly a week before her first chemotherapy treatment and had all the same fears and concerns that I had, and that was Debbie.

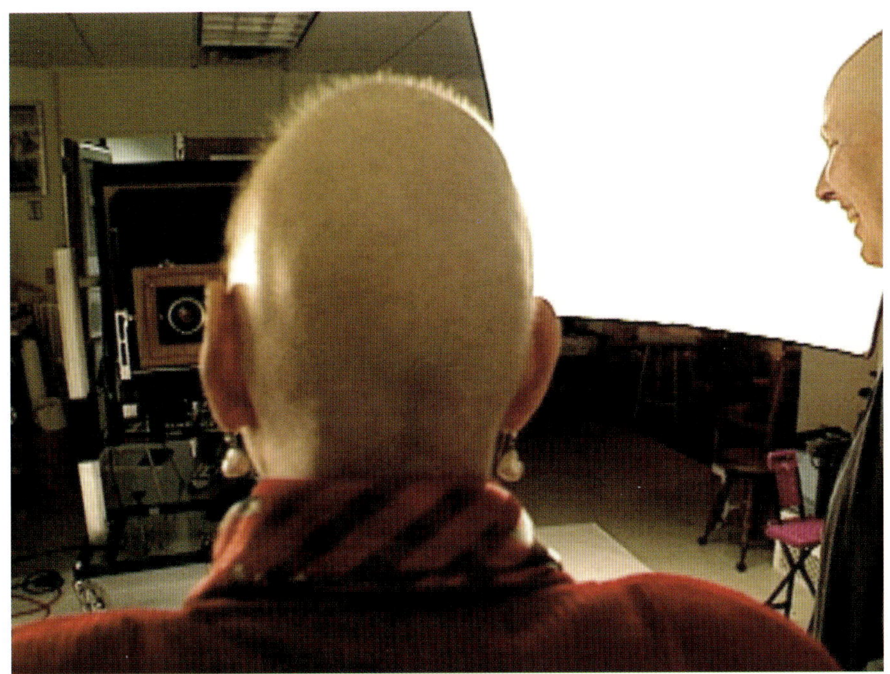

Debbie and I bonded at that point. I remember she called me that night and we talked about the group. We talked about how much better we felt after having been with the group and being with the women who were having the same treatment that we were going to have and seeing that they were actually okay. Some of them were even still working.

Our treatments were pretty much simultaneous. We finished on exactly the same day, February 19th. Actually Debbie's first treatment was a few days before mine. She called me as soon as she got home, and she said to me, Libby, it's doable.

So Debbie was somebody to joke with, even though the humor was kind of sick. We had our own little vocabulary of chemo words that we used, chemo breast and chemo mouth and chemo farts, and we talked about all the reasons why it was good not to have hair and how much money we were saving on shampoos and haircuts and how easy it was in the morning to get ready. We did a lot of laughing together, something that I couldn't do with most anybody else because most everybody else was pretty much horrified about the cancer and the treatments, but with Debbie I just let my hair down and we just made humor in what we were going through. We let our hair down.

Then through Debbie I met Carol. Carol was in the hospital with neutropenia, which is often a result of chemotherapy. I was admitted to the hospital because I had neutropenia. Debbie of course knew that Carol was in the hospital and called her on the phone and said, Libby's being admitted. I had never met Carol and I was in my hospital room, scared to death by what was happening to me, thinking that I was probably going to die because I had no white cells to fight off this infection that I had. There was a knock at the door, and a person came in with no hair, a bald person and a mask, and this is how I met Carol. She'd left the floor that she was on and she took the elevator and came down and found my room and came in to introduce herself. She immediately assuaged all of my fears and told me about what it was like and how she felt, and she was actually leaving the hospital that same night and going to Hawaii the next day. I thought, I guess I'm going to be okay after all.

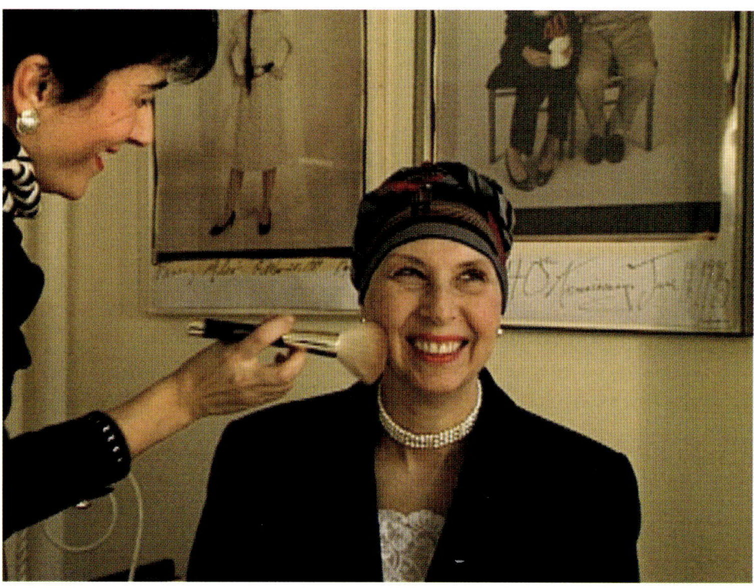

Debbie was the one who connected us with Elsa. Debbie called us and said, How do you feel about having your portrait done? A photo portrait with no hair. Bald. And I thought, yeah, that sounds pretty good. It was very difficult. I was very self-conscious of having no hair. I did not enjoy having no hair. I wore my wig faithfully every day to work. I was never seen in public without my wig. The only time I didn't wear my wig was when I went to chemotherapy, because why should I wear my wig to chemotherapy?

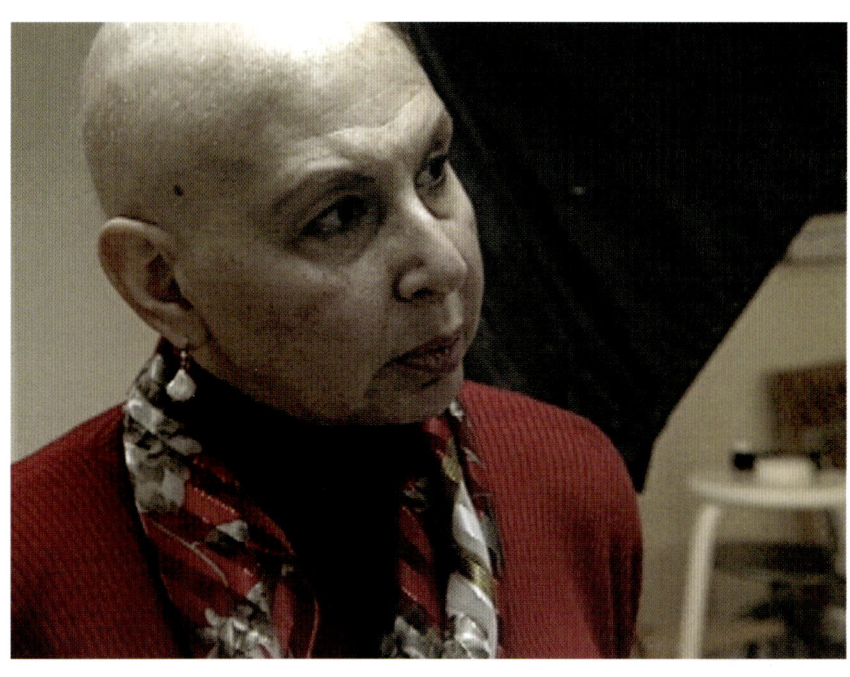

When Deb first asked me if I'd be interested in having a photograph taken of myself or having photographs taken without my hair, a portrait of a bald woman going through chemotherapy, my first reaction was, yeah, I guess so, why not? And the more I thought about it, the more I thought it would be symbolic for me because no one outside of my immediate family ever saw me without my wig or a hat. My head was always covered. My friends at work, the people that I would see on the street all looked at me like I was just, you know, another person. But the real me, the real person was a bald woman who had lost her hair because of chemotherapy. And I thought, yeah, I want to do this. I want the world to see how I am. It may not be socially acceptable for me to take my wig off at work, but this is the real me. And so I agreed to do it.

The three of us cooked up chemo-chic. Chemo-chic was going to chemotherapy looking chic. What we did was, we would buy beautiful scarves and tie them around our heads and then don a cap, a baseball cap or a hat, or something over the scarf, and look really cool and have an attitude. It was the chemo-chic attitude. And this is how I went for my chemotherapy every time and we laughed, the three of us, about chemo-chic.

I kind of felt that, well, through photography, through the photographs, we were being immortalized. And if we were lucky and we made it, fine, we had the moment captured on a photograph. And if we didn't make it, if we weren't lucky, there we were, captured in Elsa's photographs.

I try to encourage women who are newly diagnosed with cancer to join a support group and be with other women who are going through exactly what they're going through. Because there is nobody else who understands what it's like, how you feel, what your fears are. There's nobody else who understands why the first thing you think of when you wake up in the morning is, am I going to die? Am I going to be okay? And the last thing you think about before you go to sleep, am I going to die, am I going to be okay ?

LIBBY Each time I went to the hospital for my treatment or if it was for a doctor's appointment, I would identify myself as my Beth Israel Hospital number or my Social Security number. They're not interested in your name. They want to know your number so that they make sure that they give the medication to the right number. I was very solemn in this picture because I felt that I wasn't a person. I was a number being treated for breast cancer. A statistic.

ELSA Libby really wanted me take a picture of her holding a card with a number. She even brought cardboard and magic markers to my studio, along with an ugly hospital johnny, so she could draw a big number. She wanted to hold her number right across her chest. Number: I could only think of a prisoner's number or a concentration camp person's tattooed number. I couldn't get past it.

Luckily the hospital identity card was nothing to look at. Carol emptied all her charge cards. There was her drivers license. How about using that? Libby pulled out her license and so did Debbie. They looked at the pictures of themselves BEFORE the cancer. They really did look different.

LIBBY We held up our driver's licenses, which is kind of odd because on our driver's licenses we all have hair. In the portrait we're all women with no hair and we are holding up photos of ourselves with hair. But the driver's license is an identity card.

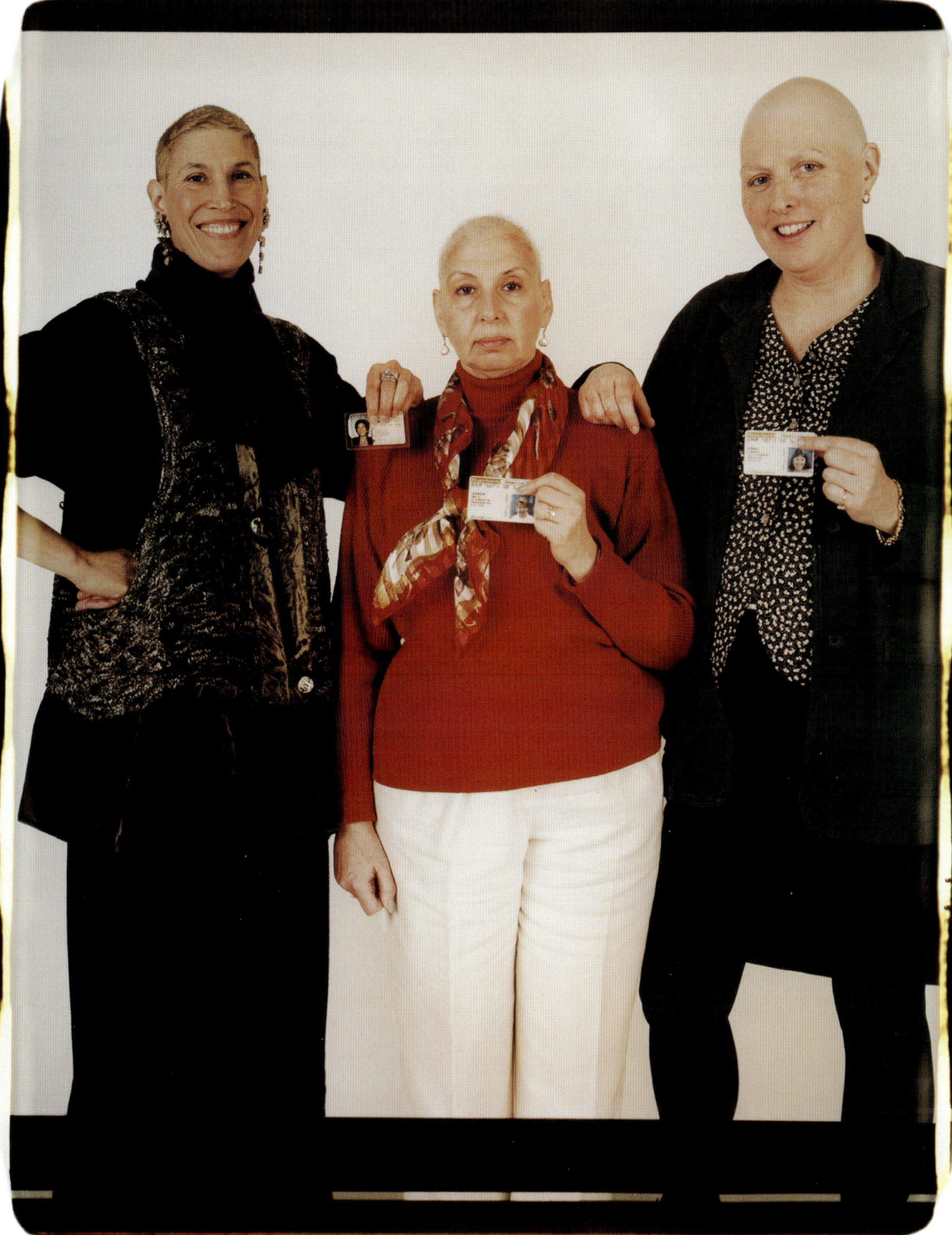

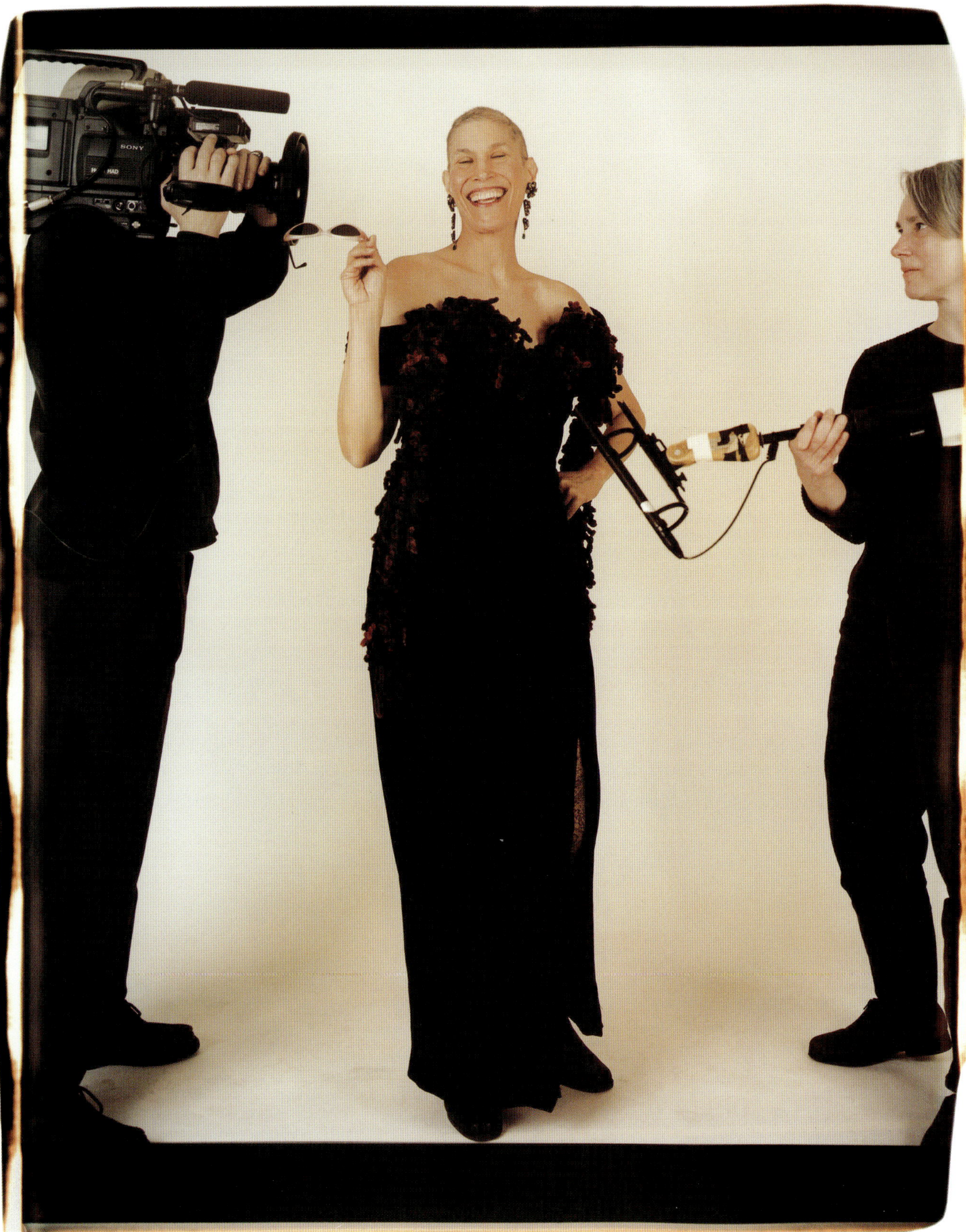
SONY

Carol Potoff

I'M AN ARTIST AND AN ART TEACHER. Libby was saying she felt like a number, and I said I feel more like a number now than I did in treatment. Then people would greet me, you know, I came to know people. They told me I look nice or something. Now I just feel like, well, did it, been there, did my treatment, done with the treatment, no big deal now, you know. I look normal now. It's kind of like, well, I had cancer, it's gone.

Now I feel like a statistic. Well, in 1997, 165,000 women were diagnosed with breast cancer, one of whom was me. Now I'm waiting to see what they say in 2002. Am I going to be one of the 35,000 who survives?

I feel much more anonymous and inconspicuous now than I did during treatment, especially because everybody was revolving around me during treatment. Now no one asks what it's like to wake up every day and go, oh, Jesus, am I okay today? What's wrong today? People don't want to know I'm still sick. I look normal.

I look fine. Well, I looked great before I had cancer. You couldn't tell by looking at me that I was sick. I just want the fear to be done so that I can really be normal.

I go once every three months to my oncologist. I see my plastic surgeon every six months. I see my radiologist every six months. I see my breast surgeon every six months. We stagger the appointments. I'm probably going up to Boston to see my doctors once every month, month and a half.

Where do I go from here with my life? Well, here's the problem. For a while I did live my life differently, and then I wake up and find that I'm in the same routine. I've gotten back into the flow of school and the same kind of frenetic pace, and I don't rest the same way that I had been, etc. The difference is now at least I'll stop myself and say, whoa, where are you going? Come back, come back, take care of yourself, relax. So that's good.

I don't know if I'll stay in teaching. I question more. What do I want to do? Life is short, so every day I think about that and as I'm going to school, I think ooh, better have fun, because who knows? Who knows what will happen tomorrow?

It's frustrating now because my health is not the same. I have more allergies now. I'm still having trouble with my bionic boob. It's a little larger than the other one, so there's a little jealousy reigning on my chest. So I have to take care of that. You know, muscle problems back here. It feels like my

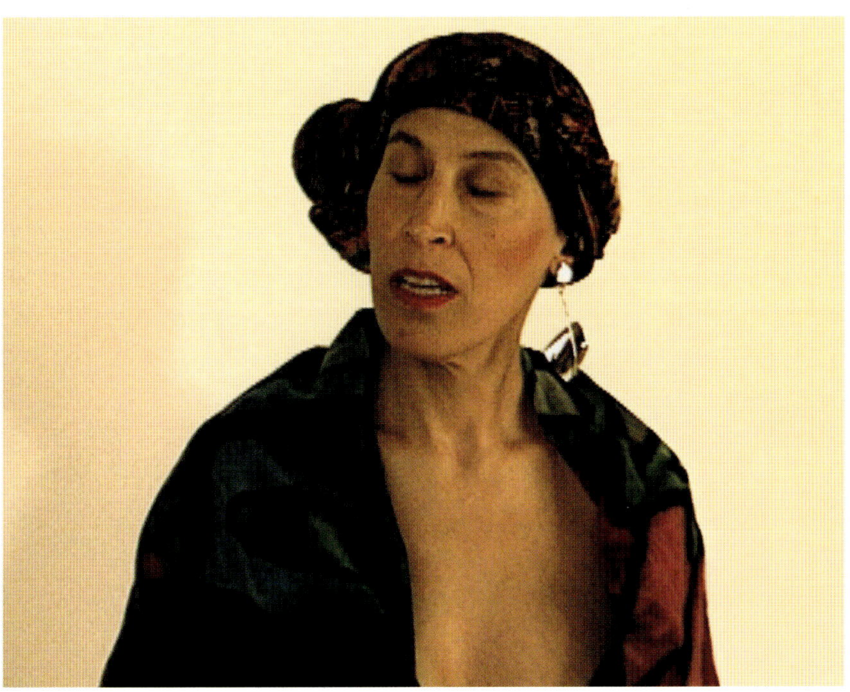

bra is too tight. So that stuff is what I have to deal with at this point in time. But I know I want to make life changes. I think I'm going to go to France for a year and live there and just do things. I don't put things off the same way I used to.

What would be the one thing I would tell another woman who was newly diagnosed with breast cancer? Actually I'd have to tell her two or three things. First off, there is life after the diagnosis and the cancer, and things get easier once she makes a decision on treatment. And the other thing I would tell her is, talk to as many people as possible who have had the treatments that she's considering. The reconstruction, the flap, an epidural, cytoxin, adriamycin, 5FU, the drugs they give you to take. Talk to as many women as possible who have gone through the process. I did talk to some people about certain parts of the procedure and not about others. Had I talked to more people, I might have changed my decisions. And I'd tell them that there's still fun out here on the other side.

Why did I get cancer? Maybe I drank too much diet soda when I was a kid. I drank it by the gallon. Maybe it runs in my family. My mother died of breast cancer. My aunts, her sisters, both had breast cancer. Maybe I'm living in a toxic waste dump. Maybe I had the wrong attitude. I was depressed. Maybe that contributed to it. Maybe the universe is trying to tell me something. I don't know. I thought I would be cured if I ate macrobiotics, but now I realize that the biscotti and cookies and the Ben and Jerry's might be just the thing to save me.

ELSA Carol never wore a wig, or at least she never took the price tags off the wigs people gave her. Being an artist with a great flair for fashion, she found unusual fabrics and made herself turbans. Originally she learned to make the turbans from a videotape at Beth Israel Hospital. But of course she took off from the video and made the turbans her own.

CAROL Losing your hair seems traumatic, but there can be some fun and wonderfully close moments. The first time I lost my hair to chemo (it's been twice now), I was freaked. I actually was in the hospital at the time and it started falling out in the shower. I called Audrey Greenway to bring the buzzer, and we had a hair-cutting party. Janie Matlaw took pictures.

I tried the wig route. Well, actually, Janie, Audrey, and I went to try them on. I was a blonde for a few minutes, and then a redhead with the long straight locks I had always wanted. Then there were the cornrows. The blonde wig didn't suit me as well as I had hoped. I looked like Patrick Swayze in *To Wong Foo With Love*. I had to agree that my natural hair color looked much more suited to me. I didn't end up buying a wig.

I preferred wearing turbans, which I tied using several scarves together. It was fun combining patterns and even putting on a pin, too. The Dana Farber has a video called "Scarves" in their lending library. I watched it with Audrey and we both wrapped ourselves in scarves that we got at Marshall's and Goodwill, trying out the different techniques.

I have to tell you that most days I felt quite exotic and lovely when I had my turban on. I became a hat-wearer, which I hadn't been. Again, great fun to try them on with a friend and laugh and carry on. Libby and I toured the cosmetic department looking for just the right purple eyeliner. Did I get creative with that!

The second time I lost my hair it was much less traumatic. I didn't feel much like wearing anything on my head. I teach art at a high school and before my hair fell out I dyed it fuschia. My students told me what kind of dyes, bleach, etc. to use, and how. Then when it started to go, a colleague at school, Jody Craven, buzzed it for me. Because many of the boys wear their hair buzzed down to the scalp, I felt pretty comfortable having my bald head uncovered, at first at school and then more and more in public. To my eyes, the world looked the same. One day at the supermarket, a woman gave me thumbs up when she saw me without any headgear.

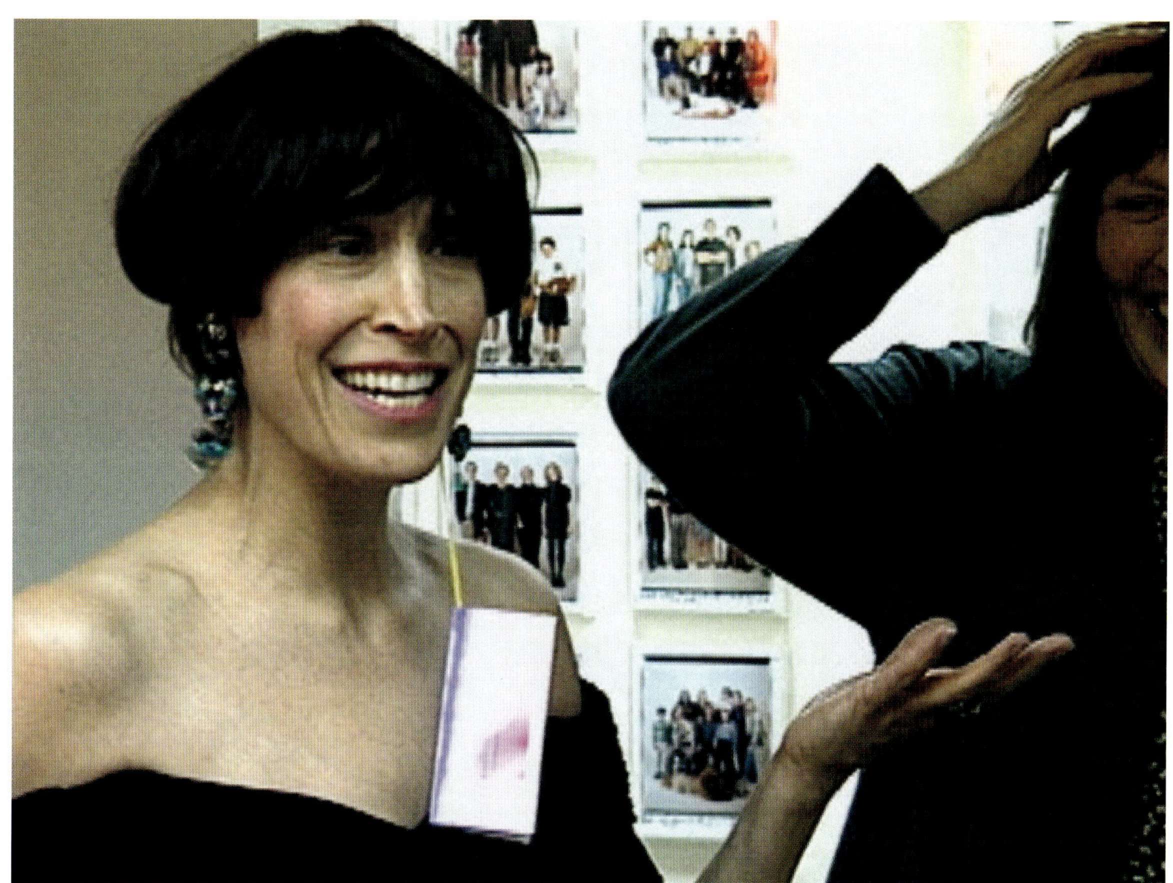

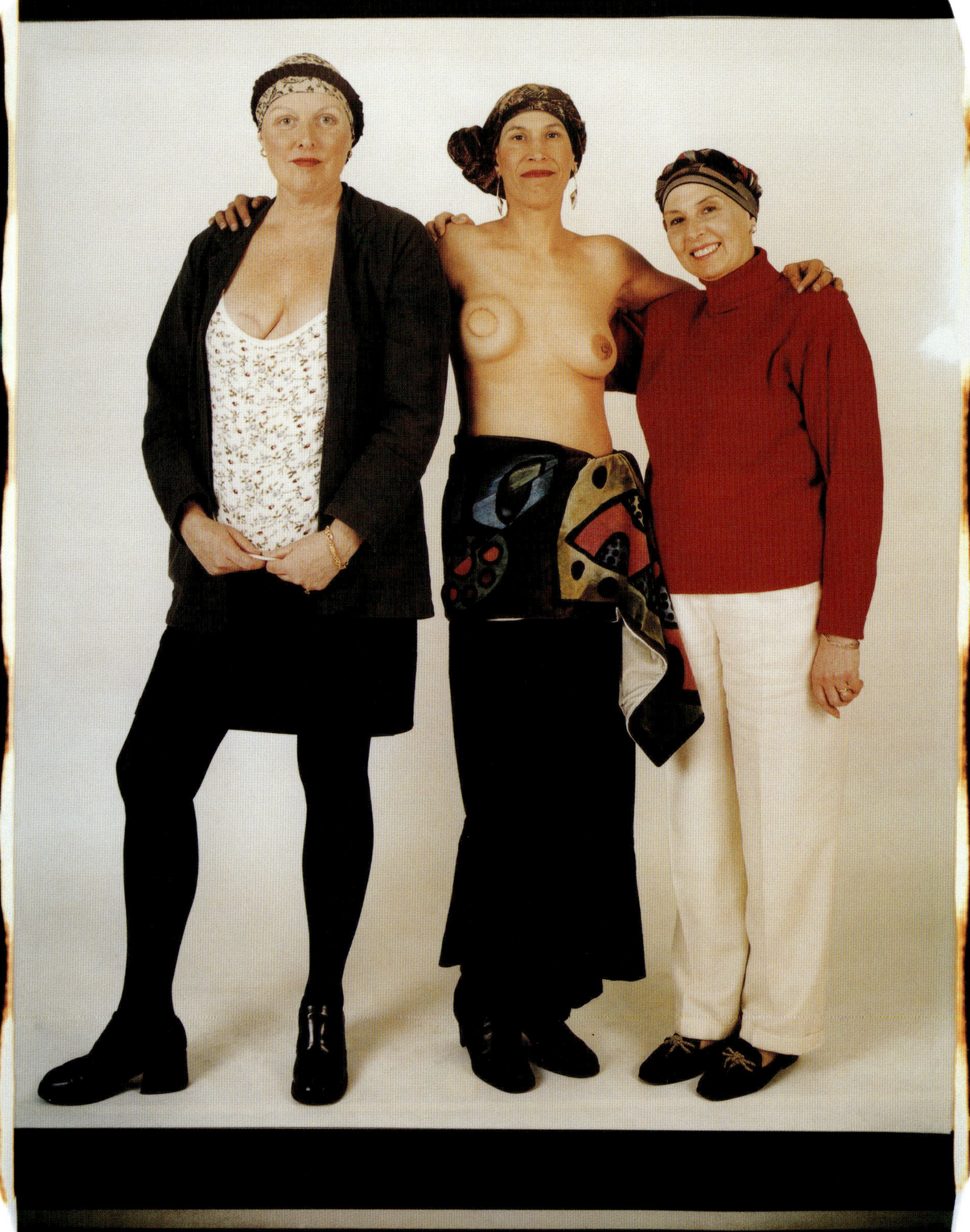

Lumpectomy

Reconstruction

Mastectomy

ELSA If you can do it, but if you can't do it, it would be fine. But it would be good if one person did it.

LIBBY I'm too modest.

CAROL Well, I'm pretty modest, but what the hell?

ELSA Okay. Well, let's see.

CAROL I got breast cancer. Every other doctor and their brother has seen my boobs.

DEBBIE Have you ever seen reconstruction?

CAROL Here it is.

DEBBIE This is what they did. This is incredible, what they did.

CAROL So, this part is just coming back.

DEBBIE So she has a scar back here.

CAROL And this was all puckered when I first came out of surgery. I thought, Oh, my God, what has he done? It was all like puckered up, so it's come down a lot, and what's happened is, see this cord? I have this cord from my arm.

DEBBIE Right. That's incredible.

CAROL But it's going away. It's much less than it used to be. It's like half the size of my armpit. This is my regular arm pit, this one. So it kind of comes through here, but it's getting better.

ELSA So now, did you have reconstruction too?

DEBBIE No.

LIBBY Mastectomy.

CAROL Reconstruction.

DEBBIE Lumpectomy.

ELSA So, Libby, are you wearing a padded bra?

LIBBY I wear a prosthesis.

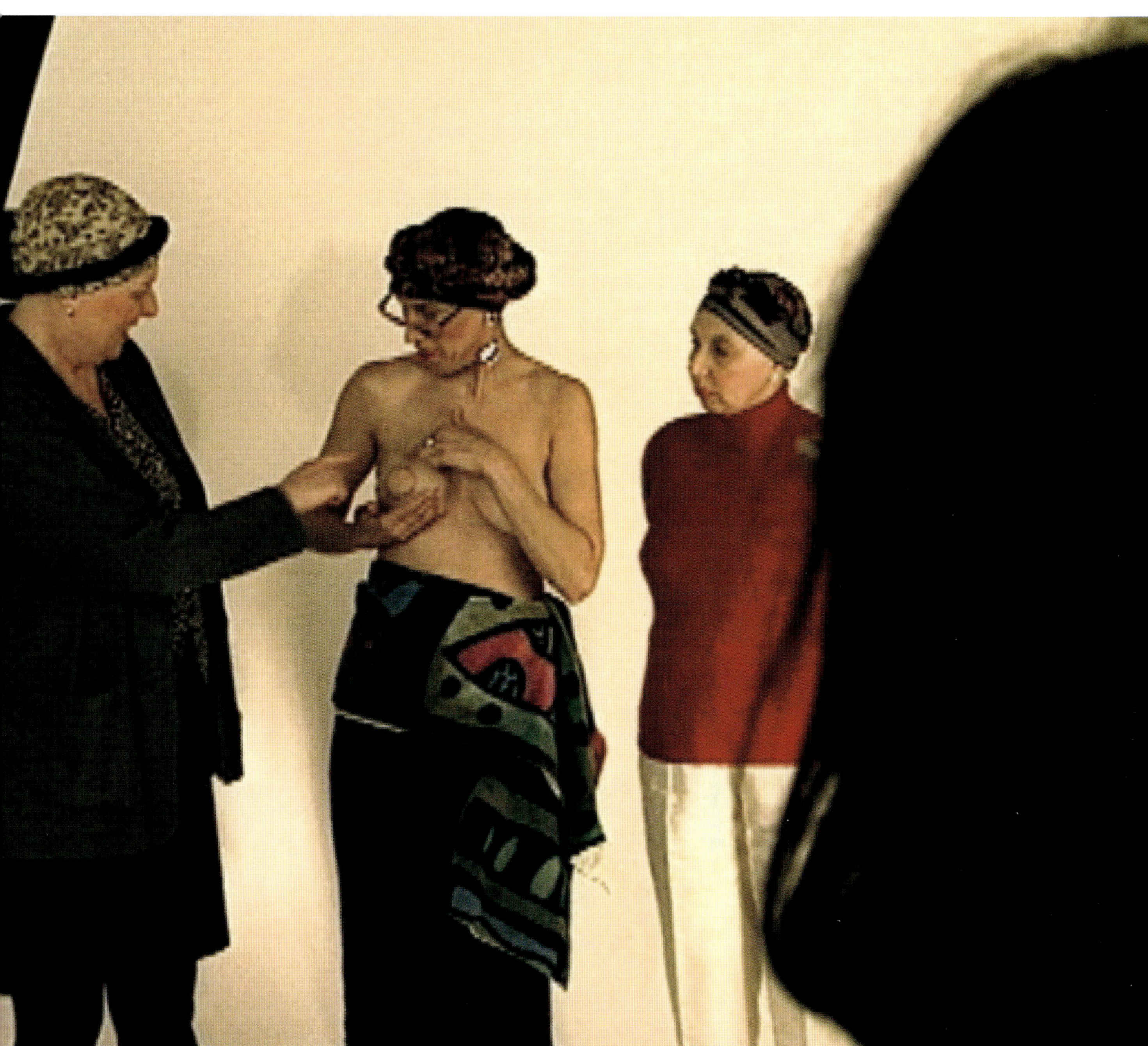

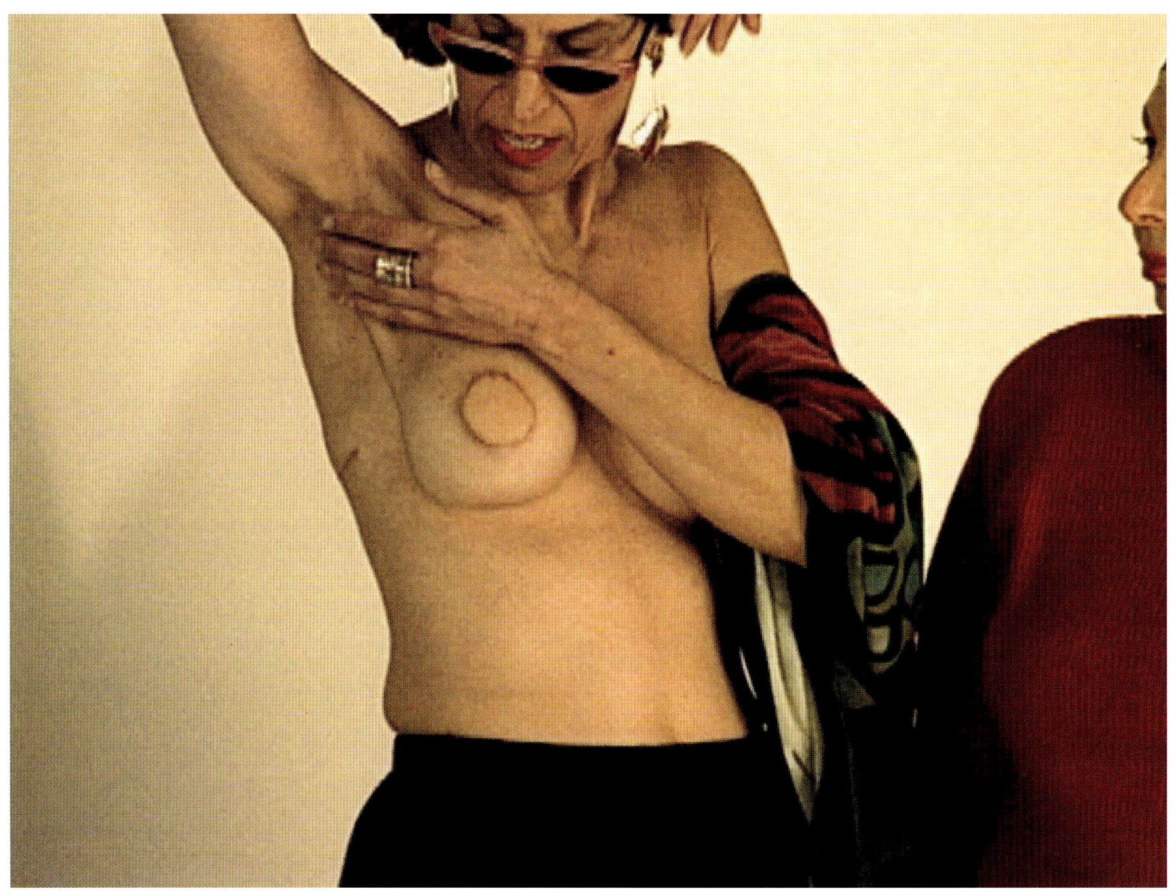

CAROL It's okay. I can do this because, see, it's not real yet. It doesn't have a nipple yet.

DEBBIE Is it all—is it all like numb?

CAROL Yeah. But you can feel. It's like a bag. But it's a bag filled with liquid, so that when you hit a high spot, doesn't it feel like there's water inside? Feel this bump, right here.

DEBBIE Oh, God!

CAROL It's weird. It's really weird. The first time I felt it, it was like, eeuw! What is that thing? So it's a little strange, still.

ELSA That isn't the old breast skin, is it?

CAROL Yeah. It's my skin.

DEBBIE It's her skin. The only thing that isn't hers is where the nipple was.

CAROL This is from my back. This is from this scar here.

ELSA I see.

CAROL This is the back skin. And then they put an implant, and they took the muscle from here—

ELSA I see. I see.

CAROL —and they tunnel it under, and flap it up in front. It's amazing what they can do.

DEBBIE How weird.

ELSA So, what is yours, Debbie?

DEBBIE It's a different scar.

ELSA I mean, that's your own breast except for the little—

DEBBIE That's right.

ELSA Well, that's nothing!

DEBBIE It's nothing, right. It's just a scar.

ELSA Just unbutton your shirt.

DEBBIE Okay. Now, my lumpectomy scar's here.

ELSA Good. The scars are good. All right. Take off, take off your undershirt.

CAROL Whew. The first time my boob is out in public.

ELSA All right. Let's go.

CAROL Strange. Now, it's starting to look really round. Tell me, men design these. No offense, Bobby, but. . . . Strange. My new boob. Very strange. I think—Today was like the first day that I thought about my real one being gone.

DEBBIE Oh.

CAROL It's like, this is just, I mean, I know the outside's the same. But it's not really shaped the same. It was a pretty breast.

Bye Bye Chickens

CAROL Somehow I heard we were going to be swinging dead chickens over our heads and throwing them into the ocean, because Libby had heard of a tradition that related to this. I wasn't sure of that, so I called my friend who's Orthodox Jewish and said, what's the story on the dead chicken?

Apparently what we've done is we've taken two traditions from Judaism. One was called Tashlich, and basically what we did at *Rosh Hashana* time was cast off our sins by emptying our pockets of bread crumbs and throwing them into water. It was an act of self-purification.

Now, a few weeks later comes Yom Kippur. A tradition evolved called Kaporot. This was on the day before Yom Kippur. You swung a fowl over your head three times. It could be a rooster, a chicken, some sort of duck. But it was still alive, and what you said was, this is my substitute, my vicarious offering, my atonement. This chicken or hen or cock shall meet death, but I will enjoy a long, pleasant life of peace. Then the chicken was killed. You either ate it or you gave it away to the poor. All the sins and the bad things went with the chicken.

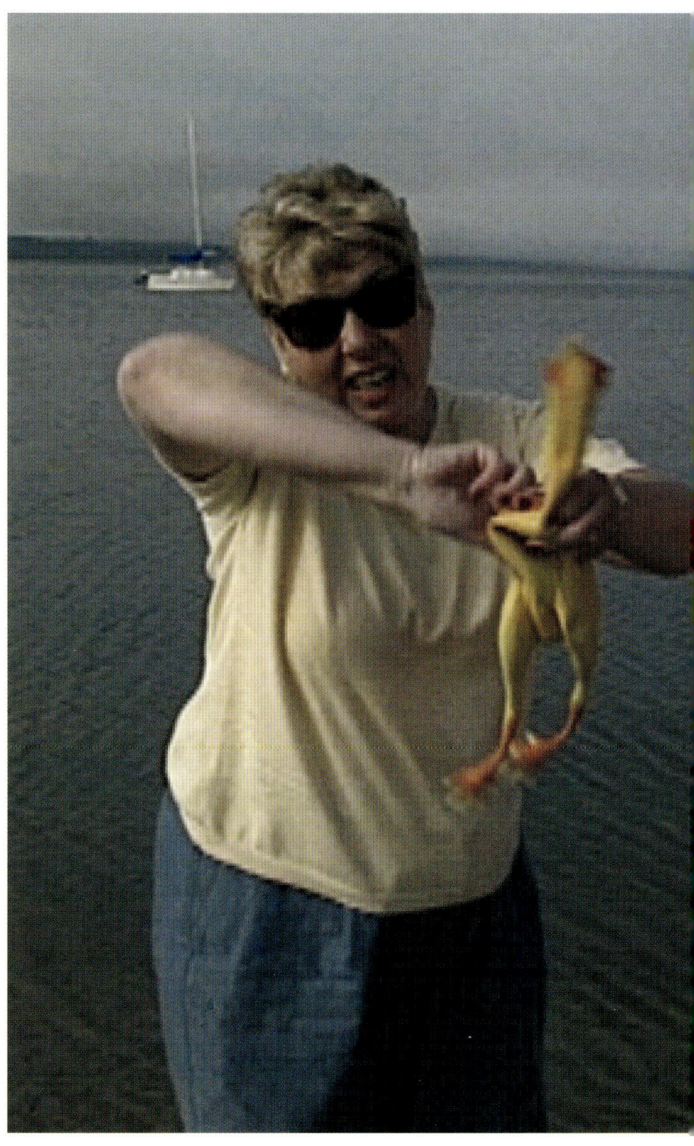

So what we did was a combination of the two traditions. We threw our chickens into the water. We used rubber chickens because I really didn't want to swing a live chicken, and certainly not a dead one, into the ocean. So thus is the life of one little rubber chicken. Bye-bye chicken, bye-bye cancer.

Bye Bye Cancer

DEBBIE Libby said, You know, Debbie, in the Jewish religion there's this tradition where you take a chicken and you swing it over your head, you throw it into the water, you say, goodbye troubles, and your troubles are gone. And I said, well, we should do that! [*laughter*] She said all right. So I went down to Carol's with Libby, and we, I brought three chickens. I wanted to do real chickens, but Carol thought they were too bloody. So I got these fake rubber chickens. [*laughter*]

CAROL So what we did was muddle two traditional ceremonies, both involved with sins and atonement and throwing objects into oceans and lakes even though our cancers had nothting at all to do with our sinning. Weird, huh?

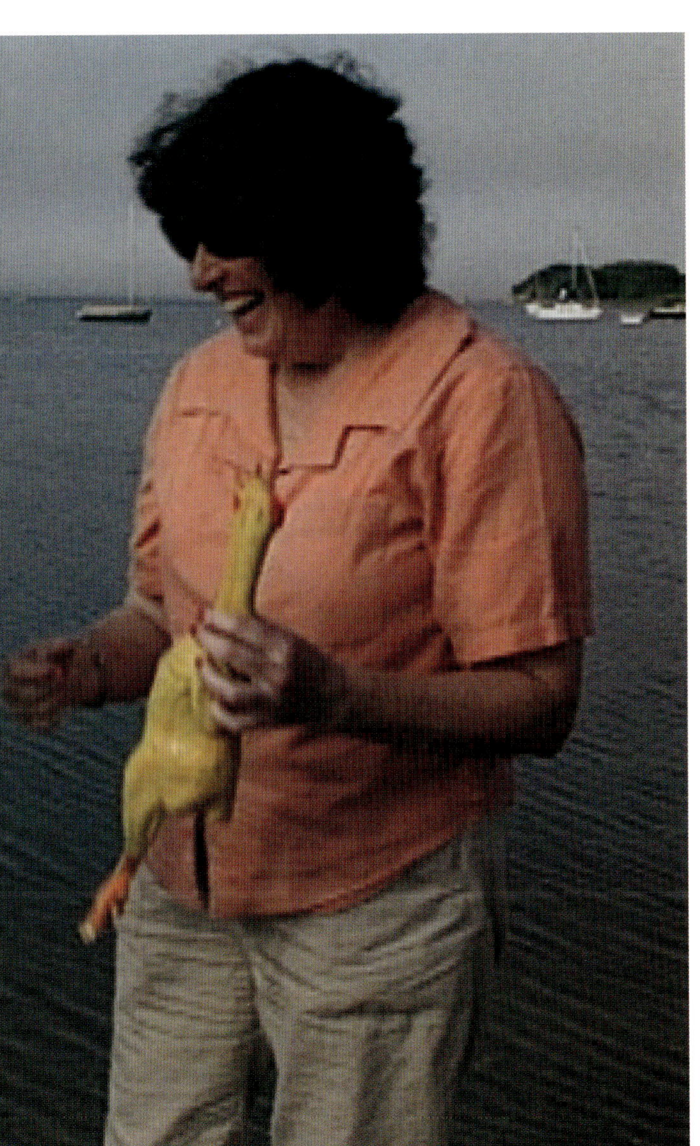

DEBBIE This represents our troubles. Our cancer is no longer. This is what Carol said she felt like.

CAROL Yup.

LIBBY Being poked and prodded.

LIBBY So now what we're going to do—

LIBBY Let's check that breast one more time. [*laughter*] Can't find anything in that one. How 'bout the other one? [*laughter*]

LIBBY Cancer's right there.
We're going to have to cut it out. It won't disfigure you much. [*laughter*]

LIBBY And then we can take a flap from your butt and put it right there, and give you a nice little breast.

CAROL This is how I felt after my surgery and things. And sometimes I feel this way, like, Oh my God, someone's kind of just hung me up.

DEBBIE Okay. This is how you feel after you have chemo, see? [*laughter*]

CAROL I think we should throw them into the water and say, cancer be gone.

DEBBIE What are we going to yell?

CAROL Yahoo!

LIBBY Yahoo!

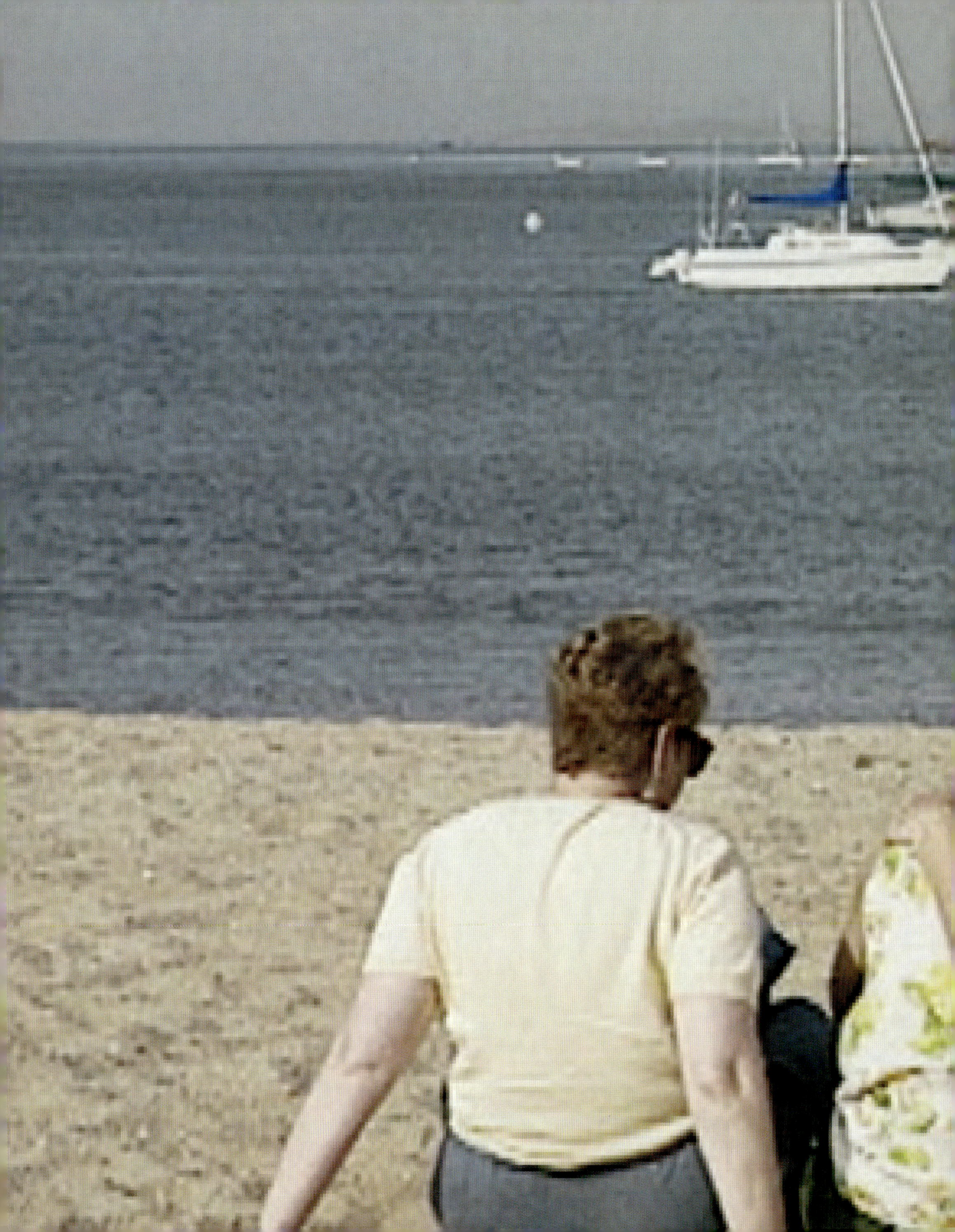

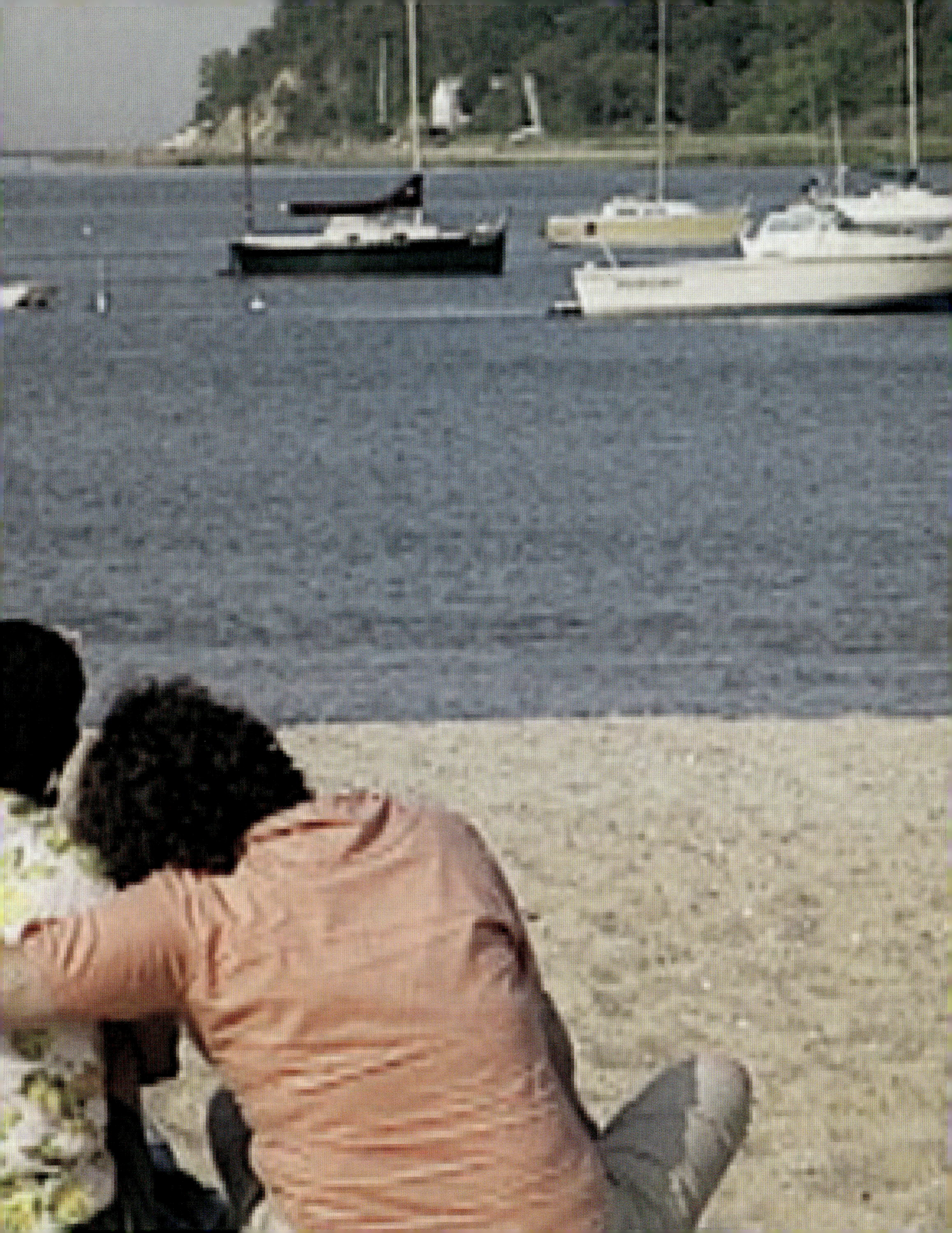

Dealing w/Bad News

From:
Libby_Levinson@idg.com
X-Lotus-FromDomain:IDG
Date:Tues,25 Sep 2001 14:17:14
Subject:Carol

Dearest Elsa,
Have you heard about Carol. Her cancer has metastasized to her lungs and her brain. She has difficulty breathing and uses oxygen. The docs are changing the chemo in the hopes they can arrest it, but it will take several weeks before they know if the new chemo is working or not. It's so scarey.

From:
DorseyTV@aol.com
Date: Tues.2 Oct 2001
23:32:13 EDT
To:elsad@theworld.com
X-Mailer:AOL 6.0 for Windows
US sub 10536
Subject: Carol

Terry's sister was in the 2nd building of the WTC in NYC on September 11th and didn't make it out.Carol is not doing very well. She has cancer all over her chest wall, in her lungs and in her brain. She's on oxygen. They're trying lots of different chemo. She's exhausted. Not good, not good at all. Let's talk soon-Debbie

---

From:
DorseyTV@aol.com
Date:Sun. 7Oct 2001
16:59:20 EDT
to: elsad@theworld.com
X-Mailer:AOL 6.0 for Windows
US sub 10536
Subject: Carol

Hi Elsa. Carol is doing very badly. I haven't talked to her, but did speak with her niece last night. Hospice is coming in sometime later this week. So, that's all I know right now. I'll let you know as I learn more- Take good care-Debbie D.

From:
Libby_Levinson@idg.com
X-Lotus-FromDomain:IDG
To:elsad@theworld.com
Date: Tue, 9 Oct 2001
13:35:42 -0400
Subject: Carol

Dearest Elsa, I wanted to update you on Carol. She was in Italy for the month of July with friends, and while she was there, the cancer began to spread. When she returned in August and saw her oncologist, the cancer had spread to her lungs and her brain. Chemotherapy has not done anything, and her body is full of the disease. She made the decision not to have any further treatments. She's at her home at the cape and her friends are with her round the clock. Don't know if she'll still be around by the 19th. I thought you'd want to know what was happening. Cancer sucks! Feeling very sad, angry, guilty, and scared all at the same time. Love. Libby.

From:
Libby_Levinson@idg.com
X-Lotus-FromDomain:IDG
Date:Wed, 28Nov 2001
11:40:59-0500
To: Elsa Dorfman
<elsad@theworld.com>
Subject: Carol

Dearest Elsa, I'll be sure to let you know when the service is. I hate cancer. Libby

---

From:
DorseyTV@aol.com
Date: Mon, 18 Feb 2002
21:21:42 EST Subject:Carol
To: elsad@theworld.com X-Mailer: AOL for Macintosh
OS X US sub 20

I got your e-mail about including Carol's dying in your book. I've thought a lot about it. I understand that you want to make the point that this is real life, that people die and it seems that a lot people we know have died lately.

After Carol died my immediate reaction was to dedicate NoHairDay to Carol. Bob was the one who got me thinking. He said NoHairDay is about life not death. I started thinking that he was right. Here we were, three bald women having poisons pumped into our body so that we wouldn't die of cancer romping around in your studio making art and celebrating that we were alive.

I feel that readers will think what's the point? One of them died and the others will probably die too. You have to keep the book full of life. The photographs you took give hope to a lot of women who have breast cancer. To read your book and to learn that Carol died will only make them feel that breast cancer is a death sentence. And sometimes it is but sometimes it's not. And we need to give those women going through diagnosis and treatment the hope that they have a good shot of making it. NoHairDay is about faith, hope friendship and courage. There should be no obituaries.

From:
Libby_Levinson@idg.com
X-Lotus-FromDomain: IDG
Wed, 20 Feb 2002
08:09:17 -0500
To: Elsa Dorfman
<elsad@world.std.com> cc:
Bob Burns
<bobburns@tiac.com>,
dorseytv@aol.com Date:
Subject: Re: Carol

It's not the way we hoped it would turn out; but we were each told the same thing by our docs: there's no cure for breast cancer; there are no guarantees that the disease will not return; it can return in 1 year, or in 5 years on in 10 years or in 18 years; or it may never return. It's a crap shoot.

Debbie and I have learned that we can't live our lives waiting for the cancer to return. If we do, then we are the losers and the cancer has won. So, we live hoping that we will be lucky and that the cancer won't return. Carol shared that hope and it was especially evident when we were in your studio being photographed. Without hope the cancer wins.

From:
Elsa Dorfman
<elsad@theworld.com>
Date: Tue, 19 Feb 2002
102918 -0500
To:debbie dorsey,
libby levinson,bob burns
Subject: Carol

I get it luvs. But I think we have to add that Carol has died. Photography is all abt death and I think abt death all the time. Nothing stays the same as it was the moment it was photographed. Photography taunts death, but of course the photograph decays and so death wins. It was my dark soul that propelled me to make you all so full of life. And the picture-making was my homage to the people who had come to my studio in the same spirit you did and who had died too soon. All the details of my photos sessions with them were with me. I couldn't tell the three of you that I was worried for you. All together we made my studio a holy place. The source of my energy was my certainty of the darkness waiting for all of us.

I can see skipping our heartbreaking news. But is nohairday only uplifting or encouraging and funny? Nohairday is abt real life. And Carol was the real thing. And the real thing happened to her. Everyone who sees nohairday or reads our book can take it. One thing I wish is that Carol's docs cd have said, hey yr cancer is so virulent, forget treatments, enjoy life. Then Carol wdn't have had to put up w/so much / shit for as long as she did. WHY DON'T THOSE DOCS KNOW MORE?

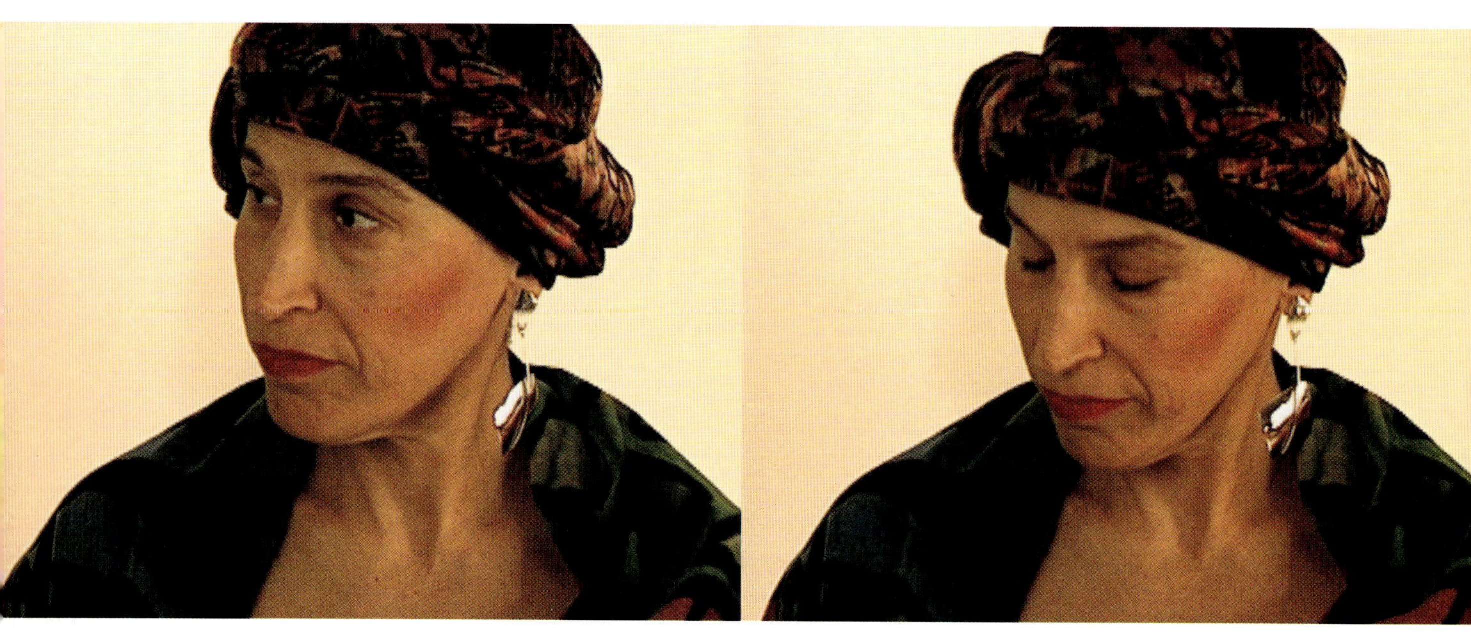

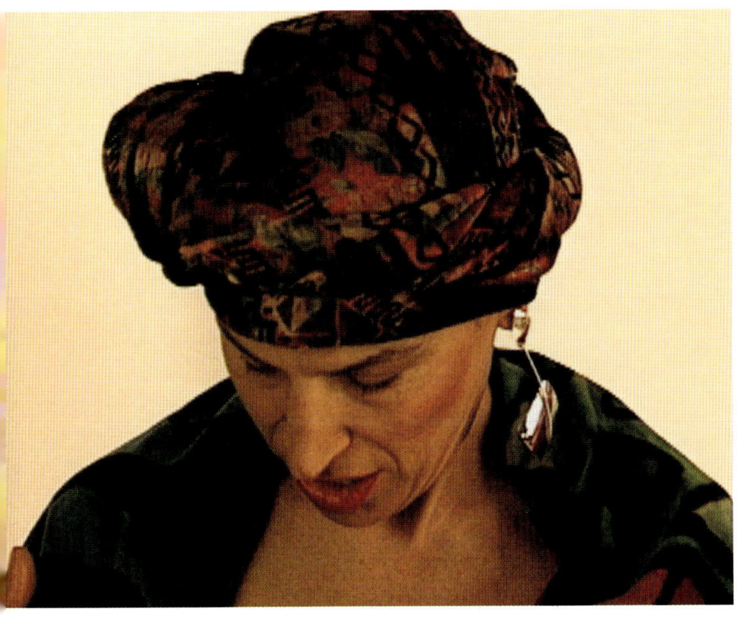

About

Elsa Dorfman is a portrait photographer and writer from Cambridge, MA. Her portraits of poets, writers and other friends were published in *Elsa's Housebook: A Woman's Photojournal* (Godine, 1974). She collaborated with Robert Creeley on the books *En Famille* (Granary Press, 1999) and *His Idea* (Coach House Press, 1975).

Bob Burns has been producing and directing science, public affairs, and educational documentaries for more than twenty years. *No Hair Day* marked a return to Bob's video roots—the very personal and experimental video art of the 1970s. Bob liked the 70s better.

Katy Homans did more than design this book. She took it under her wing and made magic. A couple of hundred books have been informed by her generous eye and her inscrutable taste. She has no favorites. She lives in Manhattan with her husband Patterson Sims and their daughters Mardet and Lally. We have been friends since 1973.

No Hair Day—the film— can from time to time be seen on the national PBS series, "Independent Focus." A VHS copy can be purchased from WGBH Video at www.wgbh.org, www.yahoo.com, www.amazon.com, www.bn.com, or by calling 1-800-949-8670. The film's web site is www.nohairday.com.

The film and the Polaroid 20 x 24 original portraits were exhibited at the DeCordova Museum and Sculpture Park, Lincoln, MA in 2000. The show was curated by George Fifield and had two godmothers, curator Rachel Rosenfield Lafo and overseer Susan Master-Karnik. Replica portraits and film were exhibited at Cape Cod Community College and the Houston Center for Photography in 2001. A portfolio of portraits was printed in *Hanging Loose* 80 and *Journal of the Hippocratic Society* (Vol.2).

Debbie Dorsey's first loves are her husband, Bob Burns, and her two children, Bobby and Georgia. Since going through the physical and emotional roller coaster that is breast cancer, she is trying her hand at stand-up comedy. She continues to make films in Boston.

Libby Levinson lives in Framingham, MA with her husband Herb and their dog Einstein. She has two adult children, Meridith and Todd. She is the Executive Assistant to the President and CEO at International Data Group in Boston, MA.

Carol Potoff died on November 28, 2001. An artist who worked in many media including yarn, she was a beloved art teacher at Nauset Regional High School in North Eastham, MA. She called her friends Darling and her cat Baby. Her alter ego was Miss Lulu, a seventy-year-old woman. Purple was her favorite color. In her school studio she had a phone that she called "a phone to God." She would say to students, if you have *that* big a problem, you can always call God. Then she would pick up the phone and say Hello God? Are you there?

Mary Panzer helped establish the skeleton of this book. In 1992 we became friends through email when she joined the National Portrait Gallery/Smithsonian as Curator of Photographs. In 2000 she moved to New York City, where she writes about photography and American culture. Her recent work includes essays on Mathew Brady, Lewis Hine, and H.C. Anderson.

Sara Blackburn, long-time Manhattan book editor, read this manuscript and offered her support and wise pencil. We were friends since 1959 and were Greenwich Village neighbors. She died October 12, 2002 of lung cancer.

Nettie Lagace is the webmaster of www.elsa.photo.net where this entire book appears and did appear in its many iterations. She graduated from Wellesley College in 1991, majoring in political science and history, and from the School of Information and Library Studies at the University of Michigan in 1995. She is a software implementation librarian at Ex Libris, which creates software for libraries. She loves inline skating on smoothly-paved paths and collecting eyeglass frames. Philip Greenspun was our match-maker: philip.greenspun.com and www.photo.net.

Jenna Webster, historian and writer, made this book a reality in ways real and spiritual. She received degrees from Harvard College and the Harvard Graduate School of Education and is a co-author of "Ben Shahn's New York: The Photograph and Modern Times," published by Yale University Press. The movies, her husband Tim and her dog Ollie are her great loves.

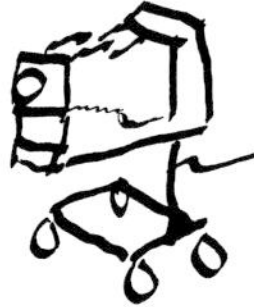

The portraits in this book were taken with a Polaroid 20 x 24" camera, one of only six in the world. (Drawing by Elsa Dorfman.)